Torn from the Headlines:
TED BUNDY

by

Scott A. Weiss

Printed by Headliner Books

Available from Website and other retail outlets

First Printing Edition, 2023

ISBN 979-8-218-30108-8

February 4, 1974
Missing Co-ed Is Sought

Police were searching for a 21-year-old University of Washington co-ed who disappeared from her U-District home at 5517 -12th Ave. NE late Thursday or early Friday. The young woman, Lynda Ann Healy, was reported missing after she failed to appear at her parents' home in Bellevue Friday evening.

Mrs. James R. Healy said her daughter was supposed to come for dinner at the family home. She also didn't show up for her morning job on a local radio station, KVI, where she gives morning ski reports.

Mrs. Healy said her daughter was last seen around midnight Thursday by a roommate. Friday morning the radio station called when Lynda didn't show up for work.

A roommate checked her room - located in the basement of the two-story house - and found Lynda's bed had not been slept in and the alarm clock still ringing.

The outside door leading to her room was open, and police said there were signs of blood on her pillow and bedding. A pink satin pillowcase and the young woman's red backpack were missing.

February 9, 1974
Police Quiz 65 On Missing Girl

Seattle homicide detectives have interviewed at least 65 people concerning the mysterious disappearance of Lynda Ann Healy, 19, missing for nearly two weeks from her U-District home.

The blue-eyed daughter of Mr. and Mrs. James R. Healy. of Bellevue, was last seen at midnight January 31 by her roommate, Joanne Testa. The two lived in a two-story house at 5517-12th Ave. NE.

Homicide Detective Lt. Patrick W. Murphy yesterday directed the public's attention to two similar, although unusual rings believed to be worn on each ring finger of the missing

University of Washington co-ed. One ring has turquoise stones erratically placed on a large, black circular field.

The other is similar except the field is turquoise with slight brown mottling in the field coloring and is minus a silver bulb on the end of the oval silver surrounding the frame.

Miss Healy is described as having long brown hair: she is five feet seven and weighs 115 pounds.

Mr. and Mrs. Healy became worried after their daughter did not arrive at their Bellevue home for supper two weeks ago. Her parents said the girl was very close to them.

The outside door to her basement room in the University District had been left open and her wallet and identification was left inside intact. Missing was a yellow knapsack and yellow ski cap. The alarm clock was still ringing.

May 23, 1974
The Case of UW Co-ed Who Disappeared

Mrs. James Healy remembers her daughter, Lynda, as an outgoing, warm 21-year-old who often sang to herself while walking down the street.

"But she might be very much different now," the mother said. "I just don't know."

Lynda Ann Healy, a fourth-year psychology major at the University of Washington disappeared Jan 31 from her basement room in a 1 ½-story older frame house at 5517 12th Ave. NE which she shared with four other UW co-eds. The next day one of the young women went into Lynda's room to discovery she was missing and the bed "unusually" well made.

There are virtually no clues, save for a few spots of fresh blood, Lynda's on the bed sheet and pillow. A pink satin pillowcase was gone as were the clothes she had been wearing the night before - blue denim jeans and a white blouse believed to have blue trim. Also missing was a red backpack.

Lynda had called her mother in Newport Hills the day before she disappeared and the two discussed a dinner Lynda had planned for her parents the following evening, Feb. 1. "I was going to bring the dessert… it was sort of a family thing," said Joyce Healy.

The missing woman's father, James Russell Healy is a salesman for the Standard Register Co. The missing person is 5 feet 7 inches tall, 115 pounds, with long brown hair, blue eyes, medium or fair complexion, pierced ears and a half-inch scar at the base of the nose bridge. Her fingers are long and slender while each thumb is shorter and thicker.

She was last seen wearing waffle stomper shoes and possibly knee-length socks, as well as the blouse and jeans.

The night before she disappeared, Lynda, along with a roommate, Joanne Testa, and a young male friend had gone to Dante's Tavern, 5300 Roosevelt Way NE, only three blocks away, for a "couple of beers," detective Ted Fonis was told. The threesome returned to the house at approximately 9:30 p.m.

The male friend left. Lynda made a phone call to an unidentified person. Then the Healy woman and Miss Testa talked in the latter's room until about 11:30 p.m. when Lynda went to her room and presumably to bed.

The following morning, Karen Skavlem, whose room is next to Lynda's in the basement, awakened at 6:30 a.m. and heard a radio alarm going on in the other room. Karen returned to sleep, but when she awoke again some 30 minutes later, she continued to hear the alarm radio and went into Lynda's room to see if she was there.

According to Fonis, the young woman's bed was made in an "unusual way." Lynda did not usually make her bed until returning from school in the afternoon.

In the meantime, a ski promotional company where Lynda worked had called the house asking if she was coming to work that day. The co-ed worked four or five mornings a week announcing ski reports over the telephones to Northwest radio stations who taped them.

The detective says the key question is whether the side door to the house was locked overnight. None of the women in the house said they could remember. A stairway leads from the side door downstairs to Miss Healy's room.

Dogs from the police department's canine unit were used Feb. 4 to search the area around the house. No leads resulted.

Then on March 30 and 31 some 70 members of the Explorer Scout search and rescue unit searched both Cowen and Ravenna Parks "with a fine-tooth comb," according to Fonis. The result was the same.

Cowen Park is a block and half from Miss Healy's home. Ravenna Park adjoins Cowen to the east. Miss Testa says she feels Lynda "was taken out of here." The roommate added: "I know her well. She wouldn't just leave."

The Healy's have hired a private detective agency, Path and Associates, to join in the search for their daughter.

Mrs. Healy said yesterday that anyone who does not want to go to the police with information about her daughter may reach her by telephone or may contact the investigative agency.

June 13, 1974
Homicide Squad Probes Case of Lost Co-ed

The mysterious disappearance Tuesday of a University of Washington co-ed, described as a "happy 18-year-old," was under investigation by Seattle police homicide detectives yesterday.

The student, Georgann Hawkins, a former high school cheerleader at Lakes High School in Tacoma, was returning to her sorority house, Kappa Alpha Theta, 4521 17th Ave NE, at 1 a.m. Tuesday via a well-lit alley when she was last seen.

She had stopped at the Beta Theta Pi fraternity house at 1617 NE 47th St. to pick up some material for a Spanish class final examination to be held Tuesday. The distance between the two houses in the same block is approximately 200 yards.

Mrs. Mary Bates, the house mother at the Kappa Alpha Theta sorority house, where Georgann lived, said there were "people all around" in the alleyway because of students staying up late studying for finals.

The missing woman is the daughter of Mr. and Mrs. Warren Hawkins of Lakewood, near Tacoma. She graduated last year from high school and was a daffodil princess in the 1973 Puyallup valley festival.

"She knew where her head was," said her mother, who works for the City of Tacoma. Her father is a branch manager for National Biscuit Co.

Georgann, a freshman, joined the sorority in September. She was intending to major in Spanish, her mother said.

"She was completely stable," said Bates. "Not one to go off by herself.

"We had an understanding," said Mrs. Hawkins. "When she left to go someplace, she would call... and when she returned, she would call us."

The missing co-ed is described as five-feet two-inches tall, 125 pounds, with shoulder-length, light brown hair and "a good suntan." She was last seen wearing a white backless T-shirt with a red, white and blue overblouse tied in front.

She also had on an expensive-looking pair of navy blue slacks and on her right ring finger was a gold band pearl ring.

In a statement yesterday, the Seattle Police Department said that "although foul play is ruled out at this time, detectives are attempting to determine if there is a link between this case and the January 31 disappearance of Lynda Ann Healy (a 21-year-old UW student) who lived in a house several blocks away."

Both women have been described by police and relatives as stable, happy young women who were almost meticulous about notifying close friends or parents when they intended to leave their residences for any period of time.

Georgann's mother said last night that her daughter "was not into the dope scene but is still a normal girl... a good student, but not a bookworm.

"She had a very outgoing personality and made friends very easily," Mrs. Hawkins said.

June 26, 1974
Women Take New Cautions in U District
Co-ed Disappearances Are Causing Concern

The side door of the two-story, green frame house on 12th Ave. NE is closed off and barred by a two-by-four.

The three young women who are living there this summer recently bought two puppies. They hope that the dogs' barking will warn them of any prowlers.

Farther east, the Kappa Alpha Theta sorority house on 17th Ave. NE is partially closed for the summer. The 19 women who are living there are all staying in basement rooms, each of which has a lock on its door.

The women at the sorority house say they are making sure someone knows at all times where they are, and they are asking their dates to walk them to the door at night to see that they get safely inside.

In these two houses lived the two University of Washington students who have mysteriously disappeared this year.

Lynda Ann Healy, 21, disappeared from her basement room in the house on 12th Avenue sometime in the early morning hours of Jan. 31.

Georgann Hawkins, 18, vanished early June 11 when she was walking back to her sorority house from a fraternity house on the end of the block. She was last seen in an alley behind the two houses. The distance from the door she walked out of to the door for which she was headed is about 150 yards.

The unexplained disappearance of these two young women has put much of the University District slightly on edge. Not only those who knew the two but also many of their neighbors have become uneasy about the neighborhood and have modified the open and easy way of living, which they say used to be characteristic of the district.

"There's no sign of any tranquility in this area anymore," said one woman who asked not to be identified.

"Everyone is a little more hesitant about speaking to strangers, and everyone is on guard almost all the time."

She said that the neighborhood has changed since she moved there seven years ago. There are so many "weird characters" on the streets, she said, that her small children have developed a "sixth sense" about strange behavior and know how to avoid it.

"I don't encourage my kids to go to the parks and play," she said. "Even adults don't walk their dogs in the parks at night anymore."

Helen Kostomarow, who was out walking her dog in the early evening, said she was "too scared" to walk the dog after dark. "We have strange people here," she said. "Once I was walking across the street when somebody took aim and threw a bottle at me from a window. Also at nighttime, people cruise around in cars and peek out at you."

Cyndy said she used to walk around by herself late at night, but she has stopped. She either finds someone to walk with her or she stays home.

"I also used to always go up and down that alley where that girl (Georgann Hawkins) disappeared," she said. "I don't do that anymore."

George Tallman said he worries about the safety of his wife and daughter and also about his property.

"This is not a good neighborhood anymore," he said. "From my house, I can see four houses that have had hi-fi stuff stolen. We used to leave the back door open, but now we keep it locked always. We've all become just a little bit more cautious."

Barb Baker now sleeps in the room from which Lynda Ann Healy disappeared. A door has been installed on that room, "better drapes" have been put up, and Barb keeps her dog with her.

The three women who were living with Lynda Ann moved out of the house for about three weeks after her disappearance and tried to find another place to live. They couldn't, so they moved back in. But this time they brought dogs with them.

Ginger Heath, one of the three, said they all are being more cautious.

"When we walk places, we go together," she said. "Also, we ride our bikes a lot of places and feel safer traveling that way."

Georgann Hawkins' sorority sisters also are being more careful.

"If I'm out late, I stay where I am and don't come home," Karen Gellatly said. "I make my dates get out of the car and walk me up to the door. And after I'm finished working, I call my roommates and tell them when to expect me home."

Leann Hunley, another Kappa Alpha Theta member, said she always checks at night to see that the windows are shut, and the doors are locked.

"I don't think, though, that things are pretty safe now because of all the publicity," she said.

On June 21, the Seattle Police Department issued a news release warning all women and "especially those who are college age and live near campus" to take safety precautions. The precautions recommended were being followed by many in the district before the police issued the news release.

They include:

- Walking with companions, especially after dark.
- Following well-lit and well-traveled streets.
- Informing someone of your route and destination.
- When returning to a parked car, checking that no one is hiding inside.
- Driving with car door locked and windows rolled up.
- Keeping house doors and windows locked at all times.
- Installing viewing devices or chain locks on front doors.
- Not allowing strangers in your homes for any reason.
- Not hiding keys under the mat.
- Listing only initials and last name in the telephone directory and on mailboxes.
- Never giving an unknown telephone caller any information about your identity.

Some young women in the U District, although aware of dangerous situations in their neighborhood, take a light-hearted approach to them.

Karen Walloch said that if she lived by herself, she would probably "be under the bed half the time.

"I get scared whenever I'm alone in the house at night," she said. "But I still walk down dark alleys. It's insane, but I still do it."

Wendy Ceis, one of Karen's roommates, said she sometimes jokingly brags about "all the chicks disappearing in our neighborhood."

Still, she said, she has taken some precautions, like walking in the middle of the road or along routes that are well-traveled.

"Sometimes I get scared in the laundromat and don't talk to anyone," she said.

Both Karen and Wendy have stories about strange people in their neighborhood. They like to tell about one stranger who came to one of their parties and was still in the house the next morning. He turned out to be harmless, they said.

Karen said she thinks there are quite a few "weird" people around. She said that one "insane guy who walks down the street yelling things to no one in particular" followed one of her friends home.

"There are a lot of weird people, but everyone ignores them," she said.

Wendy remembered one strange phone call she had.

"This guy called and said he was from Rape Relief and had a few questions to ask," she said. "He asked what I would do if I were raped, if I had ever been raped and what my bra size was. His last question made me suspicious so 1 asked him his name and hung up. Then I checked with Rape Relief and they told me that no such person worked for them."

Then there's Jeannie Terry who, with a friend, hitchhiked to Alberta, B.C. and back right after Georgann Hawkins vanished.

"Sure, 1 know that women are disappearing, and I think it's really eerie and I can't comprehend it," she said. "I'm trying not to get paranoid; I was reared in the country where we didn't even lock our doors. And I think that once I start being afraid of things like that, the city will have gotten the best of me."

July 4, 1974
Missing Co-eds - A Sinister Pattern

OLYMPIA - A sinister pattern of numbers along with similarities of looks and circumstances has emerged in the case of five missing Northwest co-eds, lawmen from Western and Central Washington were told yesterday.

The "Homicide-Missing Persons Conference," organized by Thurston County Sheriff Don Redmond, was conducted think tank-style on the campus of Evergreen State College near here. The college was the scene of one of the unusual disappearances last March 12.

The young women have disappeared off college campuses this year in Seattle, Ellensburg, Eugene, Ore. and Olympia. There have been no clues. Redmond called the meeting of some 25 officers "one long shot... beyond the normal way of doing things."

Files on the five cases and related ones were exchanged. The investigating officers in each case briefed the others. After lunch, Capt. Herbert Swindler, head of the Seattle Police Department's homicide and robbery section, led an intensive, hour-long discussion on theories and possible lines of investigation tying the disappearances together.

The pooling of possible clues among the departments was urged.

The case of Heidi Peterson, 4, missing from the front of her Capitol Hill home in Seattle since last Feb. 21, was brought up.

Swindler noted that Donna Gail Manson, a 19-year-old with brown hair and blue eyes who was reported missing after she failed to return to her Evergreen State College dormitory on March 12, disappeared 19 days after Heidi's disappearance.

Then 36 days later Elaine Rancourt, an 18-year-old with long blond hair and blue eyes disappeared from Central Washington State College at Ellensburg. That was April 17.

Again, 19 days later, Roberta Kathleen Parks, 20, also with blonde hair and blues eyes, was reported missing from the University of Oregon at Eugene.

After another 36 days Georgann Hawkins, 18, disappeared from an alley behind her sorority house near the University of Washington. The former Puyallup Daffodil princess and high-school cheerleader had long light brown hair and brown eyes.

Swindler, commenting on the pattern of numbers, asked the officers, "Anybody here know anything about numbers."

No one had an answer.

Reported missing from her home at 571712th Ave. NE, Seattle, on January 31 was Lynda Ann Healy. She had long brown hair and blue eyes.

The first of the five co-eds reported missing, her disappearance date does not fit into any number pattern.

July 17, 1974
Two More Women Reported Missing

Two more attractive young women from the Seattle area have been reported mysteriously missing - this time from the Lake Sammamish State Park area last Sunday.

Denise Marie Naslund, 19, of 4522 W. Graham St. and Janice Anne Ott, 23, of Issaquah were not together Sunday at the park. Police said the women did not know each other.

Miss Naslund, with long, light brown hair and brown eyes had come to the park Sunday with her boyfriend to join a party there. At about 4 p.m. she excused herself to go to a park rest room, and never returned. She left her car, containing her purse and some clothes.

Mrs. Ott, who works as a probation officer for King County Juvenile Court, shares a house in Issaquah with a 25-year-old female friend. Her husband is attending medical school in California.

Sunday at about noon, Mrs. Ott left a note for her roommate at the house stating, "I'll be at Lake Sammamish sunning myself."

That was the last heard from the petite, blue-eyed blonde.

Yesterday, Explorer Scouts, bloodhounds, King County and Issaquah police searched the 300-acre park at the southeast corner of the lake for some trace of the two women. Police say no trace was found.

The park is about three miles from where Mrs. Ott lives. The woman left home peddling her 10-speed bicycle. She carried a blue backpack containing refreshments and possibly lunch.

She was wearing a white sweater, cutoffs and white deck shoes.

Mrs. Ott is the daughter of Dr. and Mrs. D. E. Blackburn of Spokane and a graduate of the University of Washington.

Miss Naslund was wearing a blue halter top, cut-off jeans and sandals. She has a part-time job with dean's tops, a downtown firm supplying secretarial help.

Her boss, Doug Dean, called Miss Naslund "very reliable... she has never missed an assignment yet."

Miss Naslund is five feet four inches tall; Mrs. Ott five feet.

Both women are similar in appearance to five other young women who have disappeared under mysterious circumstances

Northwest since the beginning of the year. The five were all college or university students and were last seen either on campus or close by.

They are:

Lynda Ann Healy, 21, five feet seven inches, 117 pounds, long brown hair, missing since Jan. 31 from home at 5517 12th Ave NE Seattle. She was a student at the University of Washington.

Donna Gail Manson, 19, five feet, 100 pounds, long brown hair, blue eyes, disappeared March 12 at Evergreen State College, Olympia.

Susan Elaine Rancourt, 18, five feet-two inches, 118 pounds, long blond hair and blue eyes, missing since April 17 from Central Washington State College, Ellensburg.

Roberta Kathleen Parks, 20, five feet seven inches, 125 pounds with long blond hair and blue-green eyes. Missing May 6 from the University of Oregon at Eugene.

Georgann Hawkins, 18, five feet two inches tall, shoulder-length light brown hair and brown eyes, missing since June 11 from a University of Washington sorority house.

There were no apparent reasons for the disappearances of these young women, police have said.

King County and Seattle detectives said yesterday there was no evidence to connect the disappearances of Miss Naslund and Mrs. Ott with the five missing co-eds.

"But," said one county detective, "we're curious."

July 18, 1974
Missing Woman Seen Leaving Park With Man

One of two young women missing from Lake Sammamish State Park was seen leaving the park Sunday with a "smooth talking" man after agreeing to help him with a sailboat, a witness told police yesterday.

A small man in his late 20s with a white cast on his left arm and going by the name 'Ted' was seen talking with Mrs. Janice Ann Ott, 23, of Issaquah, at the beach, and left with the woman.

The other missing woman is Denise Marie Naslund, 19, of 4522 W. Graham St. Seattle. The two did not know each other, police said.

Many witnesses have surfaced from among the crowd at the beach Sunday, and King County and Issaquah police were busy taking statements from those who had seen the two women now missing at the beach.

According to county police, a 15-year-old female witness to the conversation described the man who talked with Mrs. Ott as "smooth talking" with "a small British accent." He was dressed in a white T-shirt and white tennis-type shorts.

Mrs. Ott was reported as telling the man, "Well OK... under one condition, that I get a ride in the sailboat."

The woman then put on her halter and cutoff pants over her black or dark blue bikini and left with the man, taking her yellow 10-speed bicycle with her.

King County homicide Sgt. Len Randall late yesterday would only say that the man seen with Mrs. Ott was "being sought in connection" with the disappearance of the Issaquah woman.

The head of the Seattle Police Department's homicide and robbery section, Capt. Herbert Swindler, said yesterday that there appeared to be no connection between the two latest missing women and the five co-eds missing from area college and university campuses.

Mrs. Ott is reported to be married to a Jim Ott who is working as an intern at a Riverside, Calif. firm which manufactures artificial limbs and braces. A spokesman at the firm said yesterday that Ott had returned to the Seattle area.

Miss Naslund, a part-time secretary, who was originally reported to have been last seen going toward a restroom at the park, was yesterday identified by a second witness as having been seen leaving the same restroom, and by a third witness as possibly being in another area of the park.

Miss Naslund had gone to the park with her boyfriend to join another couple and had walked to the restroom between 3:30 and 4 p.m.

Mrs. Ott was seen leaving the beach area with the man at about 1:30 p.m.

She lived for the past month and a half with a 25-year-old female friend, in a one-bedroom cottage on Front Street in Issaquah. Both are probation officers for the King County Juvenile Court. The roommate, Ms. Betty Stover was reportedly hospitalized yesterday after being "seriously frightened" by her roommate's disappearance, Issaquah Police Chief Ron Prosise said.

Mrs. Ott is the daughter of Dr. and Mrs. Don Blackburn of Spokane. Dr. Blackburn is an assistant to the superintendent of the Spokane School District.

The Naslund woman had left behind her car containing her purse and some clothing. Mrs. Ott had left a note for her roommate saying, "I'll be at Lake Sammamish sunning myself."

Both women had good work records.

County detectives and the Issaquah police chief yesterday watched privately made movie films of the park in hopes of spotting either the two women or the man seen with Mrs. Ott.

None was seen.

July 19, 1974
Missing Women Sought In Woods

The search for two women missing mysteriously since Sunday from Lake Sammamish State Park in Issaquah will be widened to "other wooded areas," King County Police Lt. Richard Kraske said yesterday.

Police also are searching for a Volkswagen painted an unusual shade of metallic dark brown that may have been driven by a man who, witnesses said, left the park with one of the missing women, Mrs. Janice Ann Ott, 23, of Issaquah.

No significant clues have turned up regarding the other woman, Denise, Marie Naslund, 19, of 4522 W. Graham St., Kraske said.

Mrs. Ott, who had been sunbathing at the lake, disappeared sometime between 11:30 a.m. and 12:30 p.m. Witnesses have told police she was approached by a man wearing a cast on his left arm who said his name was "Ted" and asked her to help load a sailboat on top of his car.

"Ted" had reportedly approached other women in the park before speaking to Mrs. Ott. He was described as a man in his late 20s, about 5 feet 6 inches tall, with a medium build and long blondish-brown hair, wearing white tennis shoes, socks, shorts and a T-shirt. He is reported to have a "slight" British accent. Miss Naslund, who was visiting the park with her boyfriend, disappeared after leaving a park restroom shortly after 4 p.m.

Mrs. James R. Healy of Bellevue. The mother of Lynda Ann Healy, 21, a University of Washington co-ed who has been missing since Jan. 31, said yesterday that an anonymous person has added $1,000 to the reward being offered for Miss Healy's safe return.

That reward now totals $2,000, Mrs. Healy said.

July 22, 1974
Women Jittery At Sammamish

Women sunbathers gathered in groups with other women, men and families, but the beach at Lake Sammamish State Park yesterday was noticeably void of women alone.

"I'll never come out here alone again," 13-year-old Julie Turnell vowed, in the aftermath of last Sunday's disappearance of two young women from that park, and the consensus of other women interviewed on the beach indicated the same.

Family and company picnics filled the picnic area with frisbees, baseballs and barbecues, but the beach was thinly populated for a hot Sunday afternoon.

Park Ranger Donald Simmons said that he expected yesterday's crowd to be an average Sunday size of about 17,000. He was puzzled by the light turnout at the park's beach this weekend.

One female hitchhiker, dressed in a bright pink bikini top and blue jeans, said she was not afraid of hitchhiking in front of the park. She then pointed to a gun hidden inside her beach blanket.

Another bikini-clad woman on the beach carried a switchblade. Groups of women wandered in and out of the restroom, while men waited outside to make sure their companions returned safely. One of the missing women, Denise M. Naslund, 18, was last seen leaving a restroom. The other woman, Janice Ott, 23, was last seen walking toward a stranger's bronze colored Volkswagen.

"I'm not too scared," Larry Gormley said, looking at his wife, "but I sure have been looking at VW's."

"It's scary coming out here," his wife Stephanie added. "I think next time I'd like to change at home instead of in the park's dressing rooms."

Lynn Seaborn, a sunbather, worked with Mrs. Ott at the King County Courthouse. She and her sister Kitty admitted they were scared to be there although they go to that beach often.

"We're not going to the bathroom by ourselves!" Lynn, 24, said emphatically.

"It's really deserted here today, and the police aren't usually down on the beach," Kitty, 22, said as she pointed to a police boat piling up to shore.

One young man did not seem quite as concerned as his female companion who is the news director of Bellevue Community College's radio station.

"Well, it bothered me," exclaimed Judy Linn, who monitored the sheriff's reports on the missing women from the radio station. "The other missing co-eds bother me even more."

"Well, I keep it on my mind all the time now," Jill Brebberman said as she watched her two little girls play in the sand. "I used to let them go to the restroom together, but now I go with them."

Two young single men said that the incident would not stop them from approaching and meeting single girls on the beach.

One 40-year-old woman, reading a book alone on the beach, laughed and said that she had been going to that beach for 15 years and was not afraid.

While the people at the park enjoyed the sunny weather, divers searched about a mile of the Issaquah Creek with no results. Others searched a second time the areas covered Saturday south of Interstate 90 around Cougar and Squak Mountains.

Patrolman Ken Wardstom of the King County Police, who has coordinated the search, said that search would be suspended late yesterday.

The homicide division will now review the information already gathered. Additional searches will be scheduled to follow any new leads, Wardstrom said.

July 26, 1974
Another Sketch Made Of Kidnap Suspect

King County Police issued yesterday a third version of the sketch of a man called "Ted," sought in connection with the disappearance of one of two women from Lake Sammamish State Park July 14.

Janice Ott, 23, one of two women who disappeared from the park Sunday, was seen walking toward the man's car.

Police said the changes of the sketch reflect additional information from witnesses who said they saw the man.

County police said two psychiatrists gave them a possible "character trace" of the man, which opened some "new avenues of investigation." It was not made public.

Mrs. Ott and Denise M. Naslund, 18, haven't been seen since that Sunday at the beach. Families of both young women have offered $1,000 rewards for information on their whereabouts.

July 28, 1974
$5,000 P-I Reward
Where Are Heidi And Six Women?
Disappearances Baffle the Police

Six young women and a girl, 4, have disappeared in the state since Jan. 31 in a chilling chain of incidents that has sent baffled police to psychiatrists and even to psychics in search of clues.

It is the biggest mystery of its kind in the state's history.

"It's as if the earth opened and swallowed them," said Seattle Police Capt. Herbert Swindler, whose homicide and robbery section is cooperating with other law-enforcement agencies in the state in hopes of solving the disappearances.

Police have only one real clue - a man who called himself "Ted," who apparently left Lake Sammamish State Park July 1 with Janice Ott, 23, Issaquah, one of the missing. She hasn't been seen since and neither has "Ted," despite exhaustive searches of the region.

Another of the missing, Denise Marie Naslund, 19, Seattle, vanished from the same park three hours after Mrs. Ott's disappearance. As in the case of Heidi Peterson, 4, missing since Feb. 21 from the yard of her Seattle home, and in the cases of four missing state college co-eds, police have virtually no clues to Miss Naslund's disappearance.

Law-enforcement agencies cooperating in the cases discount the likelihood of one person - or one group - snatching all seven of the missing girls. They believe several persons - not in one group - are to blame.

The four co-eds all disappeared at night from campus areas. Mrs. Ott and Miss Naslund vanished in broad daylight - and from a park visited that day by 40,000 people.

Heidi's disappearance also came during daylight.

But there is gnawing fear that the disappearances could be the work of a single person, and police won't dismiss the possibility entirely. Neither will some psychologists questioned about the theory, although they tend to doubt it.

The prospect of the disappearances being a systematic series of abductions - which could continue - has made many women fearful. Co-eds no longer walk alone at night on some campuses. Visitors to recreational areas are super-cautious about strangers. Mothers in some neighborhoods don't let children out of their sight.

These are the missing, in order of their disappearances:

Lynda Ann Healy, 21, who vanished from her bedroom in the basement of an older home in the University District here the night of Jan. 31. Spots of blood - Lynda's - were found on her pillow and sheet. She was a fourth-year psychology major at the UW.

Heidi Peterson, 4, missing since Feb. 21 from the yard of her home, 2622 10th Ave. E. Daughter of Mr. and Mrs. Roy Peterson, she was seen last by her mother at 1:30 p.m. that day. Widespread searches and nationwide circulation of her picture, including the news media, have failed to turn up a single clue.

Donna Gail Manson, 19, Auburn, who vanished from the campus of the Evergreen College, Olympia, about 7 p.m. on March 13.

Susan Elaine Rancourt, 18, Anchorage, Alaska, who disappeared from Central Washington State College's campus about 9:30 p.m. on April 17 while returning to her dorm from a meeting in a hall four blocks away. A freshman, she left her laundry in a campus laundromat.

Georgann Hawkins, 18, Lakewood, who vanished about 1 a.m. on June 11 as she was returning to the Kappa Alpha Theta sorority house from the Beta Theta Pi fraternity house just off the UW campus here.

The distance between the two houses, in the same block, is only about 260 feet and the UW freshman was walking down a well-lighted alley behind the sorority and fraternity houses in the block. Other students were in the alley because it was examination time and they were up late.

Mrs. Ott and Miss Naslund, both of whom disappeared from Lake Sammamish State Park July 14, as noted earlier. In Mrs., Ott's case, the man, "Ted," asked her to help him put his sailboat atop his brown Volkswagen sedan. She was last seen about 12:30 p.m. that day, pushing her yellow bicycle to a lot where the man had his auto parked. None of the witnesses who saw both "Ted" and Mrs. Ott at the park observed her get in the car, however - nor load her bike onto the car.

There are no clues to Miss Naslund's disappearance, according to King County Sheriff's Lt. Richard Kraske. She was last seen in a restroom about 4 p.m. with an unknown woman in a bikini.

(An Oregon State University co-ed from California, Roberta Parks, 20, vanished from that campus on May 6. Authorities there feel she may have left of her own accord and wasn't abducted. Nevertheless, her disappearance remains unexplained.)

There are many ironies about the flurry of disappearances. Miss Hawkins, a former Puyallup Daffodil Festival princess, vanished at a time when she had everything going for her.

As her mother put it:

"She was a winner - it seemed as though someone had strewn roses along her life path…"

Georgann was near-sighted and that night had left her glasses and contact lenses in her sorority house. She'd stopped at the fraternity house to pick up some examination material for that day.

Her mother said Georgann couldn't see any distance without the glasses or contacts and would have to walk right up to people to identify them.

Windows in the fraternity and sorority houses were open and a youth yelled Georgann's name down the alley, the mother said. She added:

"Whoever took her could have learned her name that way - called to her from the shadows and…"

Mrs. Ott, who worked in King County Juvenile Court, was a very sympathetic Person, say those who know her, and it may have been her undoing. King County Sheriff's Lt. Richard Kraske says she's "the type, that would take in stray dogs and cats."

"Ted" apparently stirred her sympathy because he wore his left arm in a cast and sling - and he grimaced with "pain" now and then, even holding the arm with his right hand, witnesses told police.

There is a possibility that "Ted" might be a Canadian because witnesses said he seemed to speak with an English accent. In addition, he said he hurt his arm playing racquet ball - a game rarely played in Seattle but popular in Vancouver, B.C.

Royal Canadian Mounted Police officers are investigating seven slayings in Canada, but they do not believe at present there is any link between the slayings in Canada and the disappearance of six young women in Washington.

Witnesses say "Ted" was in his 20s, about 5 feet, 6 inches tall. He was of medium build, tanned and with blondish-brown hair that partly covered his ears. They said he was very friendly and an engaging conversationalist.

He asked as many as 10 women to help him load the sailboat on his car. None - except apparently Mrs. Ott - would go to Issaquah with him, where he said the sailboat was. Another woman, 22, did walk as far as the car - thinking the boat was there - but refused to go to Issaquah with the man, Kraske said.

Mrs. Ott had gone to the park alone on her yellow, 10-speed bicycle. She was last seen pushing the bike toward "Ted's" car - but no one saw her get into the vehicle. No trace of the bike has been found. Mrs. Ott's father, Don Blackburn of Spokane, has posted a $150 reward for its return. Rewards also have been posted for some of the missing persons.

Another irony: Lynda Healy wanted to be a psychologist, explored human behavior. Now, police have had to go to psychiatrists and psychologists to get a "profile" of her abductor or abductors. The "profile" helps them understand the type of person they're seeking.

The Post-Intelligencer asked two Seattle psychologists if they thought one person could be responsible for the disappearances. Both responded but asked their names not be used. The first said:

"On the surface, it would seem it couldn't be the same person because of differences in some of the cases. But I wonder if there really are differences.

"Did the co-eds vanish at night because the same 'help me' approach was used on them? Such an approach could catch them to drop their guard. If the fellow made this approach at Lake Sammamish, it's quite possible he could have done it at night…

asked for help in getting something into his car, lifting something or moving an object.

"It's conceivable that, emboldened by his nighttime success, he came out into the daylight in the latest two apparent abductions."

The other psychologist agreed that the night successes could make an abductor "more arrogant." He said:

"I would assume anyone who does this to women has a deep-seated fear of rejection… and is very disappointed in a mothering relationship. In approaching the women, he could be saying 'I need your help, mother me - but I'm going to get you.' This could be combined with sexuality as well."

Mrs. Hawkins, mother of the Daffodil festival princess, says:

"I can't understand why no one has heard anything or found anything of these girls." She voiced fears of white slavery and drug rings.

Mrs. Hawkins recalled that after a traffic accident had killed a relative, she told Georgann:

"I never want to stand by your grave. Let me know where you're going, where you are, when you'll return."

Her daughter did all those things, the mother said - and her disappearance in the 260-foot stretch of that alley thus is all the more baffling.

The lack of clues confounds cooperating law officers. Capt. Swindler said police feel they're up against an extraordinary type of abductor. He is apparently not the common variety who seizes, attacks - possibly kills - women, then flees, not bothering to conceal the evidence very well with the result that police could expect, to find the victims or other evidence shortly.

Police have all but ruled out any chance the seven missing persons disappeared of their own accord. None gave any indication of such intent; all had definite plans for the next day.

No cries for help were heard in any of the cases - although people were nearby. The girls - except young Heidi - were similar in the respect that all were young women between the ages of 18 and 23 and wore their hair in the longer style. But there were sharp differences in heights (the range was from 5-

feet to 5-feet, 7-inches), color of hair, eyes and general appearance.

The home from which Lynda Healy disappeared on Jan. 31 is 10 blocks northwest of the alley from which Georgann Hawkins vanished on June 11. While the alley is well-lighted and at times well-populated, the street running in front of the house where Miss Healy stayed is dark.

So is an alley behind the home. A side door to the house led to bedrooms of Lynda and another girl who slept in the basement. The other girls in the house are sure Lynda "was taken out of here." The side door may not have been locked that night.

Lynda's mother says:

"She didn't leave on her own - unless she received a blow on the head - and has something like amnesia."

Lynda's voice was familiar to thousands of persons in the Seattle area because she gave skiing reports over radio stations.

Miss Manson's mother, Marie, dismisses any chance her daughter left on her own. Donna phoned home the night before she disappeared and there was nothing out of the ordinary. "We talked about her coming home for spring vacation," the mother said. She said her daughter has shown some interest in the study of magic: friends told police she was interested in the occult.

Mrs. Eleanor Rose, mother of Miss Naslund, said the girl had an argument with her boyfriend, who was with her at the park, just before she vanished - but the mother dismisses that as a factor in Denise's disappearance.

"Not knowing is the hardest. It would be better, I think, to know one way or the other," said Mrs. Rose of Denise's disappearance.

Miss Rancourt's case is the most similar to that of Miss Hawkins - both vanished in campus areas as they were headed for their rooms from meetings, and both had only a short way to go.

Dr. Robert S. Miller, dean of students at CWSC, said Susan's disappearance shook up the campus considerably.

July 29, 1974
Chief Hails Effort to Help Solve Cases of Missing 7

A $5,000 reward offered by The Post-Intelligencer for information concerning a chain of seven disappearances may help crack the cases which have baffled authorities, acting Seattle Police Chief Robert L. Hanson said yesterday.

Meanwhile, the police officer leading the investigation into the disappearances of six young women and a four-year-old Seattle girl disclosed that astrologists have predicted two more disappearances.

Hanson lauded the P-I's offer to pay $5,000 to the first person who comes forward with information leading to the arrest and conviction of the person or persons responsible for the disappearances.

"The reward is great public service and we appreciate every effort in the department's behalf," he said.

Hanson expressed hope that individuals who have information about the missing women and girl, but who might before have been afraid to talk to police, will write or call the P-I immediately.

He said a $5.000 reward would help in bringing the unsuccessful investigation to the public's attention and might entice persons having knowledge of the identity of the person or persons responsible "out of the woodwork."

Several persons did call the P-I with information yesterday.

"We feel we're at a dead end as to where to go," Hanson said.

The reward announced by the P-I brings to $30,500 the amount being offered for information in connection with the disappearances which began Jan. 31 with Lynda Ann Healy, a University of Washington co-ed.

Hanson said he found it "almost impossible to believe" that someone hasn't already come forward with information as to the identity of a man driving a brown Volkswagen who may have left Lake Sammamish State Park July 14 with Janice Ott, 23, Issaquah, one of the missing.

Mrs. Ott and Denise Marie Naslund vanished the same day from a park visited that day by 40,000 people.

The total lack of clues other than the man who called himself "Ted" and who apparently left Lake Sammamish with Mrs. Ott has, Hanson said, forced police to resort to "far-out, extreme" procedures which are not normally used.

Hanson declined to name the specific measures police have taken, but one of the steps has apparently been consultation with psychics and astrologists.

Capt. Herbert Swindler, whose homicide and robbery section is cooperating with other state law enforcement agencies in attempting to solve the disappearances, confirmed yesterday that astrologists are being used in the investigation.

Two of three astrologists consulted have concurred in a prediction that one woman or more will disappear on an upcoming weekend, Swindler said.

The astrologists, some local and some from out of town, have, Swindler said, "detailed some dates on which they feel more disappearances will occur."

Swindler refused to disclose the dates astrologists have given for fear that apprehension among area women, already made jumpy by the prospect of more disappearances, might increase.

The day on which a third astrologist predicted another woman would disappear has already passed without any new disappearances being reported, he said.

Swindler refused to "completely discount" the information which astrologists have provided. He said the department will monitor events on the days named in the predictions very closely.

"If another girl disappears on those days," Swindler said, "it will blow my mind."

Swindler indicated that King County Police officers, who along with Seattle Police are investigating the disappearances, have made contacts with psychics.

King County Police investigators could not be reached yesterday for comments on the contacts referred to by Swindler.

Swindler refused to discuss any other of the "far-out, extreme" methods which police are using in hopes of unearthing new clues. He said publicity could jeopardize their effectiveness.

The missing are: Ms. Healy, who vanished Jan. 31 from her apartment in the University District; Heidi Peterson, 4. Missing since Feb. 21 from the yard of her home at 2622 10th Ave. E.; Donna Gail Manson, 19, Auburn, who vanished from Evergreen College, Olympia.

Susan Elaine Rancourt, 18, of Anchorage, Alaska, who disappeared from the Central Washington State College campus in Ellensburg on April 17; Georgann Hawkins, 18, Lakewood, missing since June 11 from a University District neighborhood; and Mrs. Ott and Ms. Naslund, both of Issaquah.

July 30, 1974
Missing 7: The Search for Information

Fifty-four people have provided information on the disappearance of six young women and a four-year-old girl since The Post-Intelligencer posted a $5,000 reward two days ago.

No new evidence as to the whereabouts of the missing persons has turned up. The information is being evaluated and investigated to see if any of it can provide leads to a solution to the baffling disappearances.

Most of the calls, one of which came from as far away as Ketchikan, Alaska, were from people offering information on Janice Ott, 23, and Denise Naslund, 19, who both disappeared from Lake Sammamish State Park July 1.

Mrs. Ott was seen leaving the park with a slender young man called "Ted" who reportedly drove a bronze or brown Volkswagen sedan.

Other calls concerned Heidi Peterson, 4, who disappeared from the front yard of her Seattle home Feb. 21.

Still other calls related to encounters that young women in the area have had with unidentified men - many of whom drove VWs.

One University of Washington co-ed, for example, said she spoke Thursday night with a boyish young man whose description matched that of the elusive "Ted."

She was walking along Roosevelt Avenue in the University District when a late-model VW swerved across the street and parked on 42nd St. The driver, 20 to 25 years old, with bleached blond hair, stepped out and asked her for directions to an address.

He continued to engage her in conversation until a large man with a German shepherd dog appeared on the street. Then the young man abruptly left.

It may have been an innocent meeting. But the co-ed is convinced that the man stopped with the intention of abducting her.

Police have been given the car's license number and a full investigation will be made. In the meantime, the co-ed who made the report has been promised anonymity.

Four of the missing women are co-eds. Lynda Ann Healy, 21, and Georgann Hawkins, 18, both attended the University. Susan Rancourt, 18, disappeared from the Central Washington State College campus and Donna Manson, 19, was on her way to a concert at Evergreen State College when she was last seen.

Acting Seattle Police Chief Robert Hanson and Lt. Richard Kraske of the county Homicide and Robbery unit both said yesterday that more information is coming to light since the reward was posted.

"It's a lot more than we were getting before," Lt. Kraske said. "None of it will be shelved somewhere. We're investigating everything."

July 31, 1974
Did 'Ted' Abduct N.Y. Co-ed?

A suspect in a Syracuse, N.Y. abduction bears a strong resemblance to the elusive "Ted" who figured in the disappearance of at least two local women, police here learned yesterday.

The two are among six Washington women who have mysteriously dropped from sight since Jan. 31.

The Syracuse case concerns a young co-ed who vanished 20 months ago. A description and composite drawing of a young man the co-ed was last seen with is similar to that of "Ted," the man who was seen leaving Lake Sammamish State Park July 14 with Janice Ott, 23, of Issaquah.

Syracuse police said yesterday that Karen Levy, 18, a Syracuse University freshman, posted a notice on a school bulletin board asking for a ride to Monmouth, NJ where her boyfriend was attending college.

A man calling himself Bill Lacy responded. He claimed he was in Syracuse on business and was heading back to the Monmouth area.

Like "Ted," Lacy was described as being slim, clean-cut and in his early 20s. He had brown hair like Ted's. However, he was near six feet in height compared to Ted's five feet six or seven.

Capt. Herbert Swindler of Seattle Homicide and Robbery Section said yesterday that estimates of height "are frequently way off." Lacy also parted his hair differently and wore it shorter, but facial features were similar.

Miss Levy was last seen heading toward a parking lot near the Syracuse campus with Lacy. As in the cases of the missing Washington women, no trace of Miss Levy or the young man has been found.

The lead came to light yesterday from information given to The Post-Intelligencer by an Olympia resident who responded to the P-I's plea for information on the baffling disappearances.

City and county police are investigating.

The P-I has posted a $5,000 reward for information leading to the conviction of the person or persons responsible for the disappearances of the six Washington women and four-year-old Heidi Peterson.

In a related development yesterday, Ellensburg, Wash. police said an attempted abduction occurred four days after Susan Rancourt, 18, disappeared from the CWSC campus.

The information came from a library worker who told of an unidentified co-ed who was approached April 21 by a young man with his arm in a sling. The "Ted" at Lake Sammamish had his arm in a cast.

The man asked for help in loading some books in his car. The girl assisted him. Then he ordered her to start the car.

The co-ed refused and was told to get in the car. She ran to the library and told several people what had happened. The young man apparently did not try to follow her.

City and county police also will investigate the Ellensburg report. At the moment, the strongest leads in any of the disappearances relate to the so-called Ted. But the disappearances may not all be connected.

Mrs. Ott and Denise vanished from the state park on the same day, July 14. Miss Rancourt was last seen on the evening of April 17 near her dormitory.

The other disappearances involve University of Washington co-eds Linda Ann Healy, 21, and Georgann Hawkins, 18.

Donna Manson, 19, was on her way to a concert March 12 at Evergreen College near Olympia when she was last seen. Yesterday the Manson family added another $1,000 to the $500 reward offer for information leading to her whereabouts. The reward is being administered by the college.

Heidi Peterson, 4, was apparently taken from the front yard of her home on Feb. 21.

No trace of any of the missing people has been found.

Lt. Richard Kraske of the county Homicide and Robbery unit made a plea again yesterday for photographs or film taken at Lake Sammamish State Park on July 14.

"We're looking for crowd shots or parking lot shots. Anything that might have unidentified people in it. We will return any film that is given to us."

County police yesterday added six more men to the investigation to handle the leads that have been coming in since the P-1 posted its reward. The county now has 12 men working on the case who have put in more than 5,000 hours of investigation.

City police have assigned seven men to work on the disappearances.

The Reward

The Post-Intelligencer, in an attempt to assist authorities in the solution of the mysterious disappearances of six women and Heidi Peterson since Jan. 31 of this year, is offering a reward of $5,000 for information leading to the arrest and conviction of any person or persons responsible for the disappearances. This reward of $5,000 will be paid to the first person who comes forward and whose information leads to the first conviction.

Write any information to "P-1 Reward," The Seattle Post-Intelligencer, Sixth and Wall, Seattle 98111, or phone directly: 622-2000, Ext. 201.

The P-I's reward raised to $31,500 the amount being offered in connection with the disappearances. The other $26,500 has been offered by families and friends for the safe return of all seven missing persons - Heidi Peterson, $15,000; Lynda Healy, $2,000; Janice Ott, Denise Naslund and Susan Rancourt, $1,000 each; Georgann Hawkins, $5,000, and Donna Manson, $1,500.

August 2, 1974
Bicycle Is Being Sought In Missing Woman Case

Someone in the greater Seattle area is probably riding a bicycle that belongs to the missing Janice Ott.

County police want to find the bike in the hope that it will put them a step closer to learning the fate of one of the six young women who've disappeared since Jan. 31

Ott, 23, and Denise Naslund, 19, both disappeared from Lake Sammamish State Park July 31.

Mrs. Ott was last seen pushing her yellow bike toward the parking lot in the company of a slender young who called himself "Ted."

If Mrs. Ott were abducted, it's very likely that bicycle was left or dumped somewhere, according to Lt. Richard Kraske of the county Homicide and Robbery Unit. "If we can locate it and find out where it was left, we can probably find out something about what happened to Janice Ott."

Mrs. Ott's parents have posted a $150 reward for the return of the bike. Police said yesterday they're not interested in prosecuting anyone who came across an abandoned bike and rode off with it. They just want the bike and to find out where it was left.

The Post-Intelligencer has offered a $5,000 reward for information leading to the conviction of the person or persons responsible for the disappearance at the six woman and four-year-old Heidi Peterson.

Police describe the bike as being very similar to the one pictured in today's P-1. There are only two differences. Mrs. Ott's bike had no fenders. And unlike the bicycle pictured here, the Ott bike had a chain guard.

The bicycle is a yellow "Tiger" brand made in Taiwan. It's fairly common brand name in this area, however, Mrs. Ott's model had been discontinued.

It's a 10-speed girls model with racing handlebars wrapped with black vinyl and has dual-control handbrakes that are pulled from the middle of the handle bars.

The bike may have been painted by now, police said. A Tiger bike is easily identified by 12 inches of chrome on the bottom of the forks where the frame connects to the front wheel axle. A possible serial number P-290 is stamped either on the bottom of the crankcase or the right side of the vertical bar extending from the crankcase to the seat.

The vehicle has a narrow seat covered with quilted black vinyl. The 27-inch tires are gum wall mounted on chrome rods.

The bicycle cost $85 to $95 new. A comparable new model would cost in the $100 to $110 range today.

Ted, who had his left arm in a cast extending over his elbow, reportedly asked Mrs. Ott to help him unload a boat on his car. Mrs. Ott agreed, and the pair were last seen walking toward the parking lot with Mrs. Ott pushing the bike.

Ted is described as being in his mid-to late 20s, five-foot-seven to eight, 160 lbs. with brown, neck-length hair. We had an athletic build, a dark tan and spoke with a slight English accent.

Ted may have been driving a Volkswagen beetle painted an unusual medium shade of brown.

Police do not know if Miss Naslund also was contacted by Ted. Anyone with knowledge of the bicycle or Ted may call the nearest police jurisdiction or the P-I.

August 3, 1974
Women Warned: Become Warier

Police investigating the disappearance of six Northwest women urged yesterday that women attending crowded outdoor Seafair activities this weekend, beware of strangers.

"The beaches and parks are going to be crowded," according to Lt. Pat Murphy of the Homicide and Missing Persons Division.

"I hope young women will be wary about solicitations from strangers. It wouldn't be advisable for them to go off somewhere alone with someone they've never seen before.

The warning was issued in connection with the disappearance of six young women in the past two months.

Two of them - Janice Ott, 23, and Denise Naslund, 19 - disappeared from a crowded Lake Sammamish State Park July 14.

Mrs. Ott was last seen pushing her yellow bike toward the parking lot in the company of a slender young man calling himself "Ted" who had his left arm in a cast extending over his elbow and reportedly drove a brown Volkswagen.

King County police describe "Ted" as a man with an athletic build and a dark tan with neck-length brown hair parted in the middle, about 5-feet-7 or 8, 160 pounds and in his mid to late 20s. He is said to have a slight European or Canadian accent.

The Post-Intelligencer has offered a $5,000 reward for information leading to the conviction of the person or persons responsible for the disappearance of the six women and four-year-old Heidi Peterson.

In a related development, a Central Washington State college co-ed has told authorities of having an encounter in Ellensburg with a man fitting Ted's description on April 17, the night Susan Rancourt, a Central co-ed, disappeared.

Police also have an earlier report of a similar encounter in Ellensburg from another co-ed on April 21, four days after Miss Rancourt's disappearance.

Authorities said both reports are similar in that a young man with a cast or a sling on one arm persuaded the women to help him carry packages or books to his car, described by one of the women as a new model Volkswagen beetle with "shiny" paint. The women were not harmed and left.

Witnesses to the Lake Sammamish incident said Ted had asked several women for help in loading a sailboat on his car.

In another development Bellingham police yesterday discounted a possible connection between a reported assault there and the disappearances.

Four of the six women who vanished are co-eds. Lynda Ann Healy, 21, and Georgann Hawkins, 18, both attended the University of Washington. The others are Ms. Rancourt, and Donna Manson, 19, who was on her way to a concert at Evergreen State College when she was last seen.

August 4, 1974
Many Offer Search Clues

Over 160 people have provided information on the disappearance of six young women and a four-year-old girl since The Post-Intelligencer posted a $5,000 reward seven days ago.

Police are evaluating and investigating the information to determine if any of it holds a clue to the baffling disappearances. No new evidence as to the whereabouts of the missing persons has turned up.

Most of the information has come from people offering information on Janice Ott, 23, and Denise Naslund, 19, who disappeared from Lake Sammamish State Park on July 14.

Mrs. Ott was last seen pushing her yellow bike toward the parking lot in the company of a slender young man who called himself "Ted."

King County police describe "Ted" as a man with an athletic build and a dark tan with neck-length brown hair parted in the middle, about 5-feet-7 or 8, 160 pounds and in his mid to late 20s. He is said to have a slight European or Canadian accent.

Other calls have concerned Heidi Peterson, 4, who disappeared from the front yard of her Seattle home Feb. 21.

Very little, however, has turned up regarding the disappearance of four college co-eds.

Lynda Ann Healy, 21, and Georgann Hawkins. 18, both attended the University of Washington. Susan Rancourt, 18, vanished from the Central Washington State College campus and Donna Manson, 19, was on her way to a concert at Evergreen State College when she was last seen.

The only new clue involves a Central co-ed who says she encountered a man fitting Ted's description in Ellensburg on April 17, the night Susan Rancourt disappeared.

Police also have an earlier report of a similar encounter in Ellensburg from another co-ed on April 21, four days after Miss Rancourt's disappearance.

Authorities said both reports are similar in that a young man with a cast or a sling on one arm persuaded the women to help him carry packages or books to his car, described by one of the women as a new model Volkswagen with "shiny" paint. The women were not harmed and left.

Witnesses to the Lake Sammamish incident said Ted had asked several women for help in loading a sailboat on his car.

King County police have added six more men to the investigation to handle new leads, bringing to 12 the number of county officers on the case. They have put in more than 5,000 hours of investigation on the case.

City police have assigned seven men to work on the disappearances. Lt. Richard Kraske of the county homicide and robbery unit said his investigators have already interviewed over 1,200 people in connection with the missing Washington women.

August 5, 1974
Missing Women: Too Few Signs Of Foul Play

One of the most vexing aspects in the hunt for clues in the disappearance of six young Washington women is the lack of evidence indicating foul play.

Blood stains were found in the bed of Lynda Ann Healy who vanished from her University District apartment on Jan. 31.

But there's no other evidence to indicate any of the other women met with violence.

"We could have 2 prime suspects sitting right in my office," said Capt. Herbert Swindler of the police department's homicide and robbery unit. "But without evidence we couldn't even book him. We'd have to have a body, a hostage - something to show he'd broken the law."

It's an entirely different story across the border in British Columbia where the Royal Canadian Mounted Police also have a case involving six women.

In B.C., it's a trail of six bodies stretching from North Vancouver to Valemount on the Alberta border. Five of the women were young and had been raped. All of them were sexually mutilated.

"We've got a bloody sick one," Sgt. Armand DeVries said yesterday at RCMP headquarters in Vancouver. "He's the worst kind of criminal. He kills wantonly after making his victims suffer. It's a horrible thing."

The murders have all occurred during the past year and police believed at least four are connected. Three of the victims were hitchhiking in the Vancouver area when they were last seen, and one was waiting at a North Vancouver bus stop. In most cases, the bodies were dumped by the side of the road.

Two of the Canadian victims haven't even been identified, but there appears to be no link between them and the missing Washington women. The body of one young woman aged 18 to 20 was found in a forest east of Penticton. The remains of a woman of about 40 were found near Valemount. She had been decapitated.

"There has never been a more extensive search in the history of the RCMP in this area," Sgt. DeVries said. "We have a 20-man squad - all experts - looking at this."

The search in Canada has been extended to known sex offenders, patients in mental hospitals and even makers of obscene phone calls. But no strong suspect has been found.

Like Washington police, the RCMP has appealed for any information that may lead to a suspect.

The Post-Intelligencer has offered a $5,000 reward for information leading to the conviction of the person or persons responsible for the disappearance of the Washington women.

To date, more than 170 people have called the P-I with information that was then turned over to police investigators. Some of it is entirely new information that provided new pieces to the puzzle.

But police have yet to find the key to the mystery.

August 6, 1974
A Puzzling Lack of Co-ed Clues

The deepest part of the mystery of the missing Northwest women is that which surrounds two University of Washington co-eds, according to investigators.

More than 175 people have offered information on six missing women and four-year-old Heidi Peterson since The Post-Intelligencer offered a $5,000 reward, July 28, for evidence leading to the conviction of those responsible for their disappearance.

But none of the informants had information on Lynda Ann Healy and Georgann Hawkins, the two missing University of Washington co-eds.

About 80 per cent of the calls and letters related to Janice Ott and Denise Naslund who disappeared from Lake Sammamish State Park, July 14. There were a number of calls on Heidi Peterson whom police believed was kidnapped from her front yard Feb. 21.

A few calls concerned Donna Manson and Susan Rancourt who disappeared from the campuses of Evergreen and Central Washington State colleges, respectively.

"But there's just nothing - no information at all on Miss Hawkins and the Healy girl," said Capt. Herbert Swindler of the police department's Homicide and Robbery unit.

"It's extremely unusual that we wouldn't get something on those girls," Swindler continued. "We're getting absolutely nothing. Even if we had a suspect, we couldn't do anything. We've got to have some evidence that a crime was committed."

Miss Healy, 21, was the first of the young women to disappear and she's the only one for which there is evidence that she may have met with violence.

Miss Healy, a senior psychology major, was alone in her basement bedroom in the University District when she was last seen on Jan. 31. Police found stains that matched her blood type on the pillow and sheets of her bed. The bed had been carefully made in an apparent attempt to hide the stains, police believe.

Nothing was missing from the bedroom and there was no sign of a struggle. Other women who live in the house have said that an abductor could have entered the basement unseen through a side door.

Miss Hawkins, 18, a former Puyallup Daffodil Festival princess, vanished from an alley about 10 blocks away on June 11.

She was returning to her Kappa Alpha Theta sorority house from a fraternity house only 260 feet away.

Other students saw her enter the alley and walk toward the sorority house. No screams were heard and there was no sign of a struggle.

What baffles Swindler and his investigators is that no clues have been found. Normally an abductor who preys on lone women attacks und sometimes kills them, then runs off without bothering to conceal the body.

Police doubt that either woman disappeared of her own accord.

August 7, 1974
7th Young Woman Is Reported Missing

A seventh young woman has been reported missing, county police disclosed yesterday.

Brenda Carol Ball, 22, of Burien was last seen June 1, according to Lt. Richard Kraske of the Homicide and Robbery unit.

The woman's mother filed a missing person report on June 17.

Kraske said the case had not been made public because Miss Ball "was known to be gone from home for a few days at a time" and there seemed to be no link with six other women who have disappeared since Jan. 31.

"The only possible connection," Kraske said, "is that Brenda's physical description was similar…" to that of Denise Naslund and Janice Ott, both of whom disappeared from Lake Sammamish State Park, July 14.

The other four missing women looked like Miss Ball in that they each had long brown hair according to city police. Georgann Hawkins, who vanished from an alley behind her University of Washington sorority June 11, was very similar to Miss Ball, city police said.

Miss Ball is described as being five feet-three inches tall, 112 pounds, with a slender build and brown eyes. Her hair hung to her shoulders.

She was last seen just before closing time at the Flame Tavern at Ambaum Blvd. SW and 128th St. SW.

Friends told police she was not with anyone in particular and she discussed going to Sun Lakes State Park in Eastern Washington with one of her roommates.

Miss Ball had been living with several women at 232 ½ 172nd St. SW for a month. She had paid her share of the June rent and apparently took none of her belongings with her.

Police said she was unemployed and was known to hitchhike when other transportation wasn't available. It was not unusual for her to be gone from home for several days at a time. Normally, however, she would call her mother if she planned to be away for more than a few days, police said.

The Post-Intelligencer previously offered a $5,000 reward for information leading to the arrest and conviction of the person or persons responsible for the six missing women.

Yesterday police urged anyone with information on Miss Ball or the other women to report it to the nearest police jurisdiction.

August 8, 1974
'Ted' Turns Up All Around

"Ted" – the light brown-haired man sought in connection with the missing woman cases – is turning up all over.

And not just in the minds of anxious Seattleites who think they've spotted him.

"We've questioned guys fitting 'Ted's' description all over town – downtown, the North side, everywhere," said Sgt. V.M. O'Neil, as the latest suspect was being whisked away for interrogation yesterday.

This "Ted" was picked up without incident at 1:30 p.m. on 1st Avenue at University Street. The suspect had blond hair and wore a cast on his left arm, like "Ted."

The "real" "Ted" was seen talking to Janice Ott at Lake Sammamish State Park shortly before she disappeared July 14. "Ted" reportedly asked her to help load a boat on his bronze or brown Volkswagen beetle.

Sgt. O'Neil said several girls, "whom yesterday's suspect was trying to pick up," called police.

"City women are uptight," he said.

The man produced identification and denied any connection with the case, the sergeant said. But he was taken to headquarters for further questioning. He later was released.

"You'd be surprised how many guys have Volkswagens like his, and how many guys have casts on the arm," he said.

Police describe the "Ted" they are seeking as being in his mid to late 20s, and five-feet seven to five-eight inches tall. He had an athletic build, was deeply tanned and the cast extended from his wrist up over the elbow.

"Ted's" hair was neck length and he spoke with a slight English accent.

August 8, 1974
UW Co-ed's Encounter With a Man Like 'Ted'

A University of Washington co-ed had an "eerie encounter" with a man who wore a cast on his leg, just half an hour before the disappearance of her friend Georgann Hawkins, the Post-Intelligencer learned yesterday.

The man, the co-ed said, matched the description of the "Ted" who was seen a month later with Janice Ott just before she disappeared from Lake Sammamish State Park. The man who figured in Mrs. Ott's disappearance, however, had a cast on his left arm.

Miss Hawkins and Mrs. Ott are among seven young women who have disappeared without a trace since Jan. 31.

Both the co-ed and Seattle police said yesterday they don't know if the co-ed's encounter and Miss Hawkins disappearance are related.

"It's another thing that's got to be investigated thoroughly," said Capt. Herbert Swindler of the Homicide and Robbery unit. "If we keep getting leads like this, one of them is going to turn into something."

The co-ed's encounter with the apparently disabled man occurred in front of the Beta Theta Pi fraternity house near the campus about 12:30 a.m., June 11. Miss Hawkins was inside the fraternity at the time. Both the co-ed and Miss Hawkins have a similar appearance. They are nearly the same height and have long, brown hair.

The co-ed told the P-I yesterday that she was on her way to the fraternity house to get some notes from her boyfriend. They were studying for a biology examination the next day.

"There was this guy on crutches with a cast and carrying a briefcase," the co-ed said. "He kept dropping the briefcase every few steps. It looked suspicious. I mean, he was kind of weird. But there were other people in the street, so I agreed to help him."

The co-ed said she carried the briefcase as far as the fraternity house. The man expressed appreciation and made no advances.

She told him she would be inside the fraternity for five or 10 minutes and would continue to help him if he was still there when she returned. He thanked her and she left him standing on the sidewalk.

As it turned out, the co-ed stayed in the fraternity for an hour and 15 minutes. There was no sign of the man when she left.

Half an hour after their meeting, however, Miss Hawkins, 18, left by the back door of the fraternity with the intention of walking 260 feet down the alley to her Kappa Alpha Theta sorority house.

She never arrived.

Other students were nearby and heard no signs of a struggle. The incident came to light yesterday when a fraternity member who heard the story called the P-I. The newspaper has offered a $5,000 reward for information leading to the conviction of the person responsible for the disappearances.

August 10, 1974
New Sketch of Suspect
Another Photo of Missing Woman Issued Too

A new composite drawing of the man called "Ted" who was with Janice Ott shortly before her disappearance July 14 was released yesterday by county police.

Police also released a new picture of Mrs. Ott clad in the cut-off jeans and belt she was wearing when she was last seen.

Mrs. Ott, who disappeared from Lake Sammamish State Park, is one of seven young women reported missing since Jan. 31.

Police said yesterday they hope the two pictures will lead to information on the whereabouts of Mrs. Ott and possibly Denise Naslund, who vanished from the park the same day. So far, police have no direct evidence that any of the disappearances are related.

The Post-Intelligencer has offered a $5,000 reward for information leading to the first conviction of a person responsible for the disappearances.

Police said the new composite drawing, the third of Ted made public, was sketched after several witnesses who saw Ted and Mrs. Ott leaving the park said down with the police artist and described again the man they saw.

The picture of Mrs. Ott came from some undeveloped film belonging to her husband Jim.

For lanky, soft-spoken Jim Ott, it's been a question of taking the days one at a time since his wife disappeared without a trace.

"I feel a definite sense of urgency to find out something – anything about where she is," Ott said in an interview earlier this week. "This has been going on for nearly a month now. Facts are becoming blurred. The trail is growing cold."

Ott, who was living in Riverside, Calif. this summer while on a University of Washington work-study program, returned to the area shortly after his wife was reported missing.

The couple planned to move to Riverside permanently in September. Ott had been offered a job there with a firm specializing in artificial limbs, Orthomedics Inc. of Downey.

Now the 28-year-old Ott spends his days going through the motions of finishing a degree program at the University and working with a member of a group organized to help find his wife, the Jann Ott Committee.

Ott declined to speculate on the probable fate of his wife or whether her disappearance is related to the other missing women.

"I just don't know what to think about it," Ott said with a heavy voice. "The police have almost no clues. I just don't have anything to go on to say for sure what might have happened."

The Otts had been married since Dec. 29, 1972. "You could say we just started on our life together," Ott said.

One of the many things that puzzles Ott is the fact that his wife's yellow, 10-speed bicycle hasn't turned up.

"If we can find it, it might help us find Jann," Ott said.

Mrs. Ott was approached at the park by a young man calling himself "Ted" who asked for help in loading a sailboat on his car. She was last seen wheeling her Tiger-brand bike toward the parking lot in the company of Ted, who has a cast on his left arm.

Ott believes someone may have found the abandoned buke and taken it home.

"I'm absolutely sure, under no circumstances, would anyone who has the bike be prosecuted," Ott declared. "If they'll just call and tell the police where it is, no charges will be pressed. All it will cause them is a little embarrassment and they can collect a $150 reward."

Ott also hopes that men at the park on July 14 who had a cast on their arm like Ted of who may have asked for help with a boat will contact county police.

"The police have a lot of random leads to chase down," Ott continued. "A phone call will just take a few minutes and it could save the police a lot of time."

The Jann Ott Committee, which now has about 100 active volunteers, has been set up to "help police in keeping people aware that these girls are missing," according to Lois Jones, a friend of Otts and one of the founders.

The committee has received some $500 in donations so far that has been deposited in the Puget Sound Mutual Savings Bank.

Fact sheets bearing a picture of Mrs. Ott have been printed by volunteers and will be sent to the new media in a several state area early next week. Posters are to be distributed as well.

The committee plans to make a similar effort on behalf of Miss Naslund and any of the other women whose parents give consent. Much of their initial organization was set up with the help of Roy Peterson, whose four-year-old daughter Heidi disappeared on Feb 21.

Mrs. Jones, who has taken a leave of absence from her job to work for the committee, said that more than 500 phone calls that have been received from people offering information or volunteer help.

"The committee will keep going until we find them," Mrs. Jones declared. "We're going to find them no matter how long it takes."

August 31, 1974
A Holiday Word to Women: Beware

A woman whose caution apparently saved her from falling victim to the mysterious "Ted" at Lake Sammamish State Park July 14 warned other women yesterday to beware of strangers over the long Labor Day weekend.

"Ted" asked Ruth (not her real name) to help him attach a sailboat to his Volkswagen bug that day at the park. Under the impression the boat was with the car at a nearby parking lot, she accompanied him there.

But when she saw no boat - and "Ted" explained it was further away - Ruth declined to go with him. She walked back to the beach area.

Shortly afterwards, she says she saw the missing Janice Ott, 23, accompanying "Ted" toward the parking lot, wheeling her yellow, 10-speed bike alongside. No trace of Ms. Ott has been found.

Denise Naslund, 18, also vanished without trace from the park, several hours later.

These two disappearances, and those of five other young women in the state and of 4-year-old Heidi Peterson of Seattle have police baffled.

"Ted" is the only real clue in all the cases - and he can't be found.

The Post-Intelligencer has offered a $5,000 reward for the arrest and conviction of any person or persons responsible for the disappearances. Families and friends also have posted rewards on all the missing persons.

The reward for information leading to the safe return of Linda Healy, 21, University of Washington co-ed who vanished from her rooming house here the night of Jan. 31, has increased through donations from $2,000 to $3,000, her mother, Mrs. James Healy, Bellevue, said yesterday.

By a strange quirk, Ruth is a former classmate and close friend of Miss Healy. However, Ruth sees no connection between Linda's disappearance and the fact that "Ted" approached Ruth at Lake Sammamish on July 14.

Ruth gave full details of her encounter with "Ted" to police when she learned of the two disappearances at the park that Sunday.

Yesterday, with the Labor Day weekend near, Ruth warned women to shun strange men and not to go on outings alone. She said women also should be cautious of other women asking for help. She explained:

"I wouldn't have gotten into Ted's car that day - even if he'd been a woman. He was smiling all the time and was so pleasant that I really felt no fear of him - it's just that I'd never go anyplace out of sight with a stranger, man or woman,"

Friends and co-workers of Jan Ott said she was of a trusting nature - which may have been her downfall. Thousands of posters with the missing women's pictures and data about them are being circulated in the state by authorities and volunteer organizations as police continue their efforts in the baffling chain of disappearances.

September 8, 1974
Hunters Discover Skeleton

Two early morning grouse hunters stumbled upon the bones of what appeared to be a young female in an isolated, heavily wooded area a mile and a quarter east of here yesterday.

King County Police, who investigated the remains, said they were satisfied the bones were not those of one of the seven missing young women who have vanished from the state this year.

Early erroneous reports that a body and four shallow graves had been discovered created a flood of rumors throughout Western Washington.

The discovery drew some 20 law enforcement officials to the site - from the King County Police Department, the State Patrol, the Seattle and Issaquah police departments - and over 30 newsmen.

The rumors of a "mass grave site" stemmed from the first reports given to the Issaquah Police by the men who discovered the bones.

"They saw some places where the dirt looked like it had been disturbed," said Capt. Nick Mackie King County commander of detectives. "We've probed and dug them up now and there are no graves."

The hunters discovered a spine and ribcage, two detached leg bones, a skull with the lower jaw missing and long shank of black hair not attached to the skull. No clothing, jewelry or other personal effects were found.

There was no immediate identification of the remains pending examination by the King County medical examiner.

However, police said the skull was small and narrow, which suggested the body was that of a woman.

The teeth of the skull were in good condition and a search of dental records will be made, police said. The present theory is that the remains are of a young hitchhiker. The police computer will be used to check runaways in the area.

The mother of Denise Naslund - who vanished along with Janice Ott from Lake Sammamish State Park this summer - arrived at the discovery site and was assured by police that the remains were not those of her daughter.

Police said since the teeth of the skull were in excellent condition, they were unlike those of Ms. Naslund, who reportedly had a poor dental history.

Police also assured the parents of Janice Ott that the body was not that of their daughter.

The area was entirely sealed off yesterday and newsmen were not allowed within a quarter mile of the site.

"We do not want anyone contaminating the crime scene," said a police spokesman.

County police yesterday were recruiting some 80 Eagle Scouts to make an "inch-by-inch grid search" today of the entire area.

"We don't feel there is any possibility of a link with the seven missing women," Mackie said, "but we're not going to leave any stone unturned."

Lt. Richard Kraske, the King County policeman who has directed the search for the seven missing girls, said it appeared the bones had been dragged down the thickly wooded bluff by animals.

Seattle newsmen who covered the story were frustrated and angry by the light security thrown around the area, just three miles east of where two women vanished this summer.

A police car was parked across an old service road leading off I-90 about 20 miles east of Seattle. The road wound back into the hills before connecting again with the highway.

State troopers were stationed on both sides of I-90 to direct the rapidly swelling traffic of onlookers who clogged the sides of the highway.

The intense interest in the discovery reflected the great public concern surrounding the disappearances of the young women, which have investigators baffled.

"What this means is we may have another unsolved homicide on our hands," said Mackie.

The Seattle Police Department and the King County Police have a joint agreement to inspect any incident that may involve the missing women. Seattle police left about 1:30 p.m. yesterday when it appeared the remains were not connected to the mysterious disappearances.

The bones were discovered at 9:58 a.m. by Elzie Hammons and Elza Rankin of Seattle. They tipped their discovery to two teenagers who were target practicing in the area, Jeff Hartsfield and Roger Darling. The four men then notified the Issaquah police.

Lt. Kraske used the incident to encourage the public "to keep calling in information regarding the missing girls."

The Post-Intelligencer has offered a $5,000 reward for information leading to the conviction of the person or persons responsible for any of the disappearances. The reward will go to the first person who provides information leading to the first conviction.

September 11, 1974
'Worst We Feared Is True'
2 Bodies Missing Women's

Two of three bodies found since last weekend near Issaquah were identified yesterday as those of Mrs. Janice Ann Ott, 23 and Denise Marie Naslund, 18, who both disappeared from nearby Lake Sammamish State Park on Sunday, July 14.

Police say they don't know how the women died.

Four additional spinal bones and a leg bone found in the same area are those of yet a third person, University of Washington anthropology professor" Dr. Daris Swindler said yesterday.

Dr. Swindler said' the additional bones "might be" those of a third woman.

That discovery prompted authorities to order a new search of the area today.

"We have no way of knowing how many remains are located at the site," one officer said, "That's why we're staying up there."

"The worst we feared is true," Capt. Joseph N. Mackie of the King' County Police Department said as he announced that the two women had been positively identified yesterday afternoon by comparing sets of teeth from the remains with dental charts.

Some clothing also has been found outside the 200-foot circle in which the bones were found, it was learned yesterday.

Eleanor Rose, Ms. Naslund's mother, learned at about 2:30 p.m. yesterday that her daughter had been identified.

"It's a terrible thing," a relative at Mrs. Rose's home said last night. "She's taking it very hard."

Mr. and Mrs. Don Blackburn of Spokane, parents of Mrs. Ott, were told of the identification of their daughter yesterday afternoon in a meeting with County Homicide Lt. Richard Kraske.

The numerous bones discovered by county detectives and volunteers over the past four days have come from 30 locations in the brush and fern-covered site.

The site is two miles east of Lake Sammamish State Park, and one and a half miles east of the center of Issaquah, several hundred yards to the north of Interstate 90.

The first set of bones - a lower jaw, a rib cage and a spinal column - were found by Elzie Hammons, a Seattle construction worker who was grouse hunting in the area early last Saturday.

When contacted last night following the identification of the remains. Hammons said, "I hope they just get the guy, or whoever did it, and put him away for good."

"Ted", the handsome young man with an arm cast seen with Ms. Ott leaving the Lake Sammamish beach area to his car that Sunday, remains at large. Capt. Mackie said he could not give out any information on the possible arrest of a suspect in the cases of the discovered bones.

Asked if an arrest was imminent, the captain said, "No, not right now."

He did add, "But we now have a crime."

There had been no evidence of foul play in the cases of the missing women until last Saturday.

In addition to the bones, police said eight tufts of human hair were found in the search area.

The decomposition and deterioration of the bodies were accelerated by animals in the area and a hot summer, police said.

Lt. Kraske, who once patrolled the area as a uniformed officer, said there were numerous coyotes in the hills outside Issaquah.

Mrs. Ott was a King County juvenile probation officer who lived in Issaquah. Miss Naslund, a part-time secretary, lived in Seattle. The two women did not know each other and were last seen at different times of day.

September 11, 1974
Police Still Seek Mysterious 'Ted"

It was probably the hot and sunny weather, with the promise of pretty girls swimming and sunbathing, that drew "Ted" to Lake Sammamish State Park July 14.

Of the 40,000 people who decided the cool lake shores were the ideal spot to spend the summer's day, the slender, soft-spoken man in his 20s was the only one to have been seen with Janice Ott before she disappeared.

Three hours after Mrs. Ott was seen walking with "Ted" towards the parking lot, Denise Naslund also vanished.

The King County police would only say yesterday that they were working on the identity and whereabouts of the mysterious "Ted," and would not comment on the progress of the investigation.

At the time of her disappearance, Mrs. Ott, 23, was sharing a house in Issaquah with a 25-year-old female friend. Her husband was working in California.

Sunday about noon, Mrs. Ott left a note for her roommate at the house that read, "I'm at Lake Sammamish sunning myself."

She was wearing a white sweater, cut-offs and white deck shoes. On her back was a blue backpack containing refreshments and possibly lunch. She pedaled to the lake on her yellow 10-speed.

Like many others, Denise Naslund, 18, drove from Seattle to spend the day by the lake. She went with her boyfriend to join a group of friends at the park for a Sunday party.

She, too, was dressed for the sun, with a blue halter top, cut-off jeans and sandals.

Around 12:30 p.m., a man calling himself "Ted" asked Mrs. Ott to help him put his sailboat atop his brown Volkswagen sedan. She was last seen pushing her bicycle to a lot where the man had his auto parked.

None of the witnesses who saw both "Ted" and Mrs. Ott at the park observed her get in the car, however - nor load her bike onto the car.

At about 4 p.m., that day, Denise Naslund excused herself to go to a park restroom. She never returned and left her car, containing her purse and some clothing.

The man seen with Janice Ott has been described as in his 20s, about 5 feet, 6 inches tall, of medium build, tan and with blondish-brown hair that partly covered his ears.

Mrs. Ott, who worked in King County Juvenile Court, was described by friends as a very sympathetic person, "the type that would take in stray dogs and cats."

"Ted" apparently stirred her sympathy because he wore his left arm in a cast and sling - and he grimaced with pain now and then, even holding the arm with his right hand, witnesses told police.

He asked as many as 10 women to help him load the sailboat on his car. None - except apparently Mrs. Ott - would go to Issaquah with him, where he said the sailboat was.

Another woman, 22, did walk as far as the car, thinking the boat was there, but refused to go with the man.

Denise Naslund - who worked for a downtown firm that supplied secretarial help - was not seen with "Ted". And until yesterday, there have been no clues as to her disappearance.

September 11, 1974
Issaquah Search Barren

A continuing search near Issaquah yesterday by 200 persons for more human remains where the bones of two Seattle-area women and a third person were found last week has not led to any major new discoveries, the King County Police Department reported late yesterday.

It was uncertain yesterday whether the search would resume today.

Some of the bones recovered during the search last week were those of Mrs. Janice Ott, 23, of Issaquah, and Denise Marie Naslund, 18, a part-time Seattle secretary. Both women had been missing from nearby Lake Sammamish State Park since July 14.

Mrs. Ott was last seen leaving the park with a slightly built young man who called himself "Ted."

September 19, 1974
No Clues Found On Other Bones

There is no way to identify the sex of a partial skeleton found with the remains of two young women near Issaquah, a University of Washington anthropologist said yesterday.

"It's impossible to make a positive identification as to whether the bones are male or female," said Prof. D. M. Swindler. 'All I could do is guess and I don't want to do that."

The third set of bones - mostly vertebrae - were found near the partial skeletons of Denise Naslund and Janice Ott on a wooded hillside east of Issaquah. Both young women disappeared from Lake Sammamish State Park July 14.

A grouse hunter found the first bones Sept. 7 and searchers subsequently found 45 to 50 bones. Ms. Naslund and Mrs. Ott were identified by dental records.

Swindler said he has returned the bones to the county medical examiner. If hip bones had been found, it would have been possible to identify the sex of the remains, he said, and a skull or jawbone would be needed to make positive identification.

Police called off the search for more remains last Monday.

Lt. Richard Kraske of the County Homicide and Robbery unit said no markings were found on any of the bones to suggest the bodies were dismembered immediately after death.

He said dogs, coyotes and rodents scattered the bones across the hillside.

September 26, 1974
Different 'Ted' In Calif.

King County police said yesterday there appeared to be no connection between a man wanted for murder and kidnaping in California and the "Ted" being sought in Western Washington for the murders of two women.

Homicide Lt. Richard Kraske said the "Ted" wanted by Santa Clara, Calif. police for the murder of one little girl and the kidnaping of another used a different method of operation from the man wanted here. Kraske said he and Santa Clara officers exchanged information yesterday.

The "Ted" sought in Washington state is wanted in connection with the murders of Mrs. Janice Anne Ott, 23, and Miss Denice Marie Naslund, 19. The bodies of the women were found two weeks ago on a hillside east of Issaquah.

Both women had disappeared July 14 from Lake Sammamish State Park. Ms. Ott was seen leaving with a man who went by the name of "Ted."

The "Ted" wanted in California has shoulder-length hair and long sideburns. He was said to have lured a six-year-old girl into his car Monday by promising to show her some rabbits. The girl was later released unharmed.

The same man is believed to have killed a four-year-old San Jose girl whose body was found last Sunday.

September 26, 1974
An Expert on Human Bones
Dr. Swindler Is a Big Help to Students, Police

Dr. Daris R. Swindler is a physical anthropologist, a teacher of comparative osteology, and once-in-a-while homicide detective.

He works out of the basement of the Burke Memorial Museum at the University of Washington. He sports a white goatee and carries the rank of full professor.

The 49-year-old West Virginian is also one of the nation's foremost experts on human bones, which makes him valuable to the students of UW and to police departments as well.

He carries no badge, but when area homicide detectives or the King County Medical Examiner's office need to know.

Age, sex and stature of a person based on the discovery of bones, they usually come to hint.

Dr. Swindler held up the half of a human pelvis (actually the combination of three bones) and exclaimed:

"There are 18 different traits (of the pelvis) that can be used to diagnose the sex of a person... the sub pubic angle is always greater than 90 degrees in a woman, and less than 90 degrees in a man."

One half of the pelvis may be as reliable in determining the sex of a person as the full skull and lower jawbone, he said.

As for judging height, or stature, Dr. Swindler maintains that the femur, or thigh bone, is most reliable. Measurements of the leg bone are run through a formula and a quantitative index. An anthropologist can come within "one and a half inches above or below the persons height."

But there are the rare cases when anthropologists are wrong.

"It's a probability thing... Something scientists don't like," he said.

The best judge of age is the fusion of bones, such as those making up the skull, or the "cranial structures" as the profession calls them. The fusion process continues from infancy until there is no trace after 45 or 50 years old.

Based on the state of fusion, Dr. Swindler said he could judge the person's age to within five to eight years.

Most recently, Dr. Swindler assisted in the identification of two women - Ms. Janice Ott and Denise Naslund - whose remains were found at a site east of Issaquah nearly three weeks ago. He also determined that four vertebrae and a piece of pelvis of a third person had been discovered at the same location.

While working on his Ph.D. at the University of Pennsylvania back in the 50s, he did similar work for the Philadelphia Police Department as well as for the FBI in Washington.

He modestly acknowledges that physical anthropologists are playing a bigger and bigger part in solving homicides these days. "We can be of help," he says.

October 16, 1974
Clark County Bones Not Those of Missing Co-eds

The skeletal remains of two young women found last weekend in Clark County are not those of the four Washington college co-eds who have, mysteriously disappeared since the beginning of the year, officials said yesterday.

The discovery of the bones brings to eight the number of young females who have either been found dead or who are believed to have been victims of foul play this year in the state. All have been in their late teens or early 20s.

Clark County Sheriff Gene Cotten said one of the skeletons is a female, 17 to 22 years old, five feet to five feet two inches tall, with light brown or blond hair and a protruding lower jaw.

The second is a female, 20 to 25 years old, five feet five to five feet seven inches tall, and with dark brown hair and possibly a reddish tint under certain light.

The bodies had been at the site for three to six months, Cotten said, and presumably brought there naked. There are no missing young women from Clark County who would fit these categories of time and description, Cotten said.

"We are not working on any suspects," said Cotten.

He said his office would get the descriptions of the women to different law enforcement agencies in the Northwest, "and people who feel they can match (the descriptions) we have requested to send the dental charts to our county coroner."

The coroner is Arch Hamilton. P.O. Box 1687, Vancouver, Wash.

The remains were examined by Dr. Daris Swindler, an anthropology professor at the University of Washington, yesterday.

The terrain and situation of last weekend's discovery - on a wooded hillside, 25 miles east of Interstate 90 and near Yacolt -

is strikingly similar to the finding of the remains of two Seattle-area women last month near Issaquah.

Denise Marie Naslund, 18, and Janice Ott, 23. disappeared from Lake Sammamish State Park July 14. They were not acquainted with each other, and they were reported missing at different times that day.

In both cases, it was a hunter who found the remains; there were no clothes or pieces of clothing discovered in the area, and the age category as well as difference in ages, was similar.

The four college co-eds whose mysterious disappearances this year remain unsolved are:

Lynda Ann Healy, 21; Susan Elaine Rancourt, 18; Donna Manson, 19; Georgann Hawkins, 18.

Thu, Oct 24, 1974
Melissa Smith still missing; police seek help in search
The Jordan Valley Sentinel (Midvale, Utah)

Midvale police have investigated dozens of leads, tips or rumors concerning the disappearance of Melissa Smith.

Melissa, 17-year-old daughter of Midvale Police Chief Louis Smith, disappeared Friday night after visiting a friend at the Pepperoni Restaurant 669 East Center St., at approximately 10 p.m.

Police have had reported sightings of Melissa from Brigham City to Richfield, but so far nothing has been confirmed.

Police are investigating all of the reports turned in. All police agencies in the state are cooperating to help locate Melissa. The FBI has started an investigation to determine if federal laws have been violated in the disappearance.

Melissa is described as five ft. three inches tall, weighing 105 lbs., with light brown hair, hazel-colored eyes, and a fair complexion. When last seen she was wearing a blue flowered blouse with a heavy navy shirt and blue jeans. She had on brown shoes with laces.

Police suspect that there may have been foul play in the girl's disappearance. They request that anyone with information about the missing girl contact a police agency as soon as possible.

Monday, Oct 28, 1974
CHIEF'S DAUGHTER FOUND MURDERED IN MOUNTAINS
The Ogden Standard-Examiner (Ogden, Utah)

The nude body of a young woman found by hunters in Summit County Sunday was identified as that of Melissa Smith, 17, daughter of Midvale Police Chief Louis Smith, officers said.

Police Lt. Derald Austin of Midvale said the police chief identified the body Sunday night as that of his daughter, who had been missing more than a week after last being seen at a Midvale restaurant.

Residents of Midvale had pledged more than $1,000 reward for anyone finding the chief's daughter. Sheriff Ron Robison of Summit County had said the girl appeared to have been shot in the back of the head and strangled. A blue nylon stocking was found near the body, he said.

He said the girl appeared to have been dead about 36 hours. An autopsy was ordered at the University of Utah Medical Center, he said.

The body was found in Tolegate Canyon by three hunters, authorities said.

November 11, 1974
Missing Bountiful Girl Hunted
The Daily Herald (Provo, Utah)

BOUNTIFUL, Utah (UPI) - An extensive air and ground search has turned up no trace of a missing 17-year-old girl who vanished Friday night.

Det. Ira Beal of the Bountiful Police Department said today that officers have no clues in the disappearance of Debra Kent, daughter of Mr. and Mrs. Dean Kent of Bountiful.

Beal said the family had gone to a play at Viewmont High School Friday night. While still at the school Mr. Kent asked his daughter to take the family car to pick up a younger brother who was at a roller-skating rink across town. She never made it to the car, according to the detective.

"We've searched the area both from the air and on foot but so far, we haven't found anything," said Beal.

Debra was described as the type of girl who would call her parents if she was going to be even 15 minutes late.

She was last seen wearing white pants and a blue flowered top with an Eisenhower jacket. She has brown eyes. long brown hair and is 5-10.

November 28, 1974
Murder victim identified as missing Salem girl
Deseret News (Salt Lake City)

The nude body of a murdered teenage girl found in American Fork Canyon Wednesday has been identified as Laura Aime, 17, daughter of Mr. and Mrs. James Aime, Salem, Utah.

Medical Examiner Dr. Serge Moore showed the 17-year-old girl died approximately one week ago from multiple blows to the head and strangulation.

Utah County Sheriff Mack Holley said Miss Aime has been missing for a month.

The parents called Holley today and came to Salt Lake with Miss Aime's dentist to make a positive identification at 11:15.

Holley said Miss Aime has "been staying with friends in various places" but the last time her parents saw her was a month ago.

The sheriff added that police were just beginning to check with friends to find who saw her last.

The body was discovered by a Brigham Young University couple hiking in an area 500 yards northeast of the Timpanogos Cave Visitor's Center. No clothing was near the scene, about 12 yards from the road behind a hill.

Area law enforcement officers planned to meet today or Friday to discuss possible similarities in the slaying of Melissa Smith, 17-year-old daughter of Midvale Police Chief Louis Smith in October. Two other cases are also involved.

Her nude body was also found with a stocking knotted around the neck, but in Parley's Summit. An autopsy showed she was beaten and strangled after being raped.

"The two appear to be linked together," said Salt Lake Sheriff's Captain Pete Hayward. He is involved in the case because of an apparent abduction attempt of still another girl in Murray.

Originally, authorities expected the body to be 17-year-oid Debra Kent of Bountiful who disappeared Nov. 8 in a suspected abduction. Dental records proved it wasn't.

Other incidents in the Salt Lake-Murray area, including Miss Kent's disappearance and the attempted abduction of the girl at a Murray shopping mall, have raised apprehension that one person was responsible for all of them.

The body was found face down on a ledge above American Fork River, only a few yards from the main canyon road.

Holley said his office had begun questioning persons about the killing but had no real suspects. "We just have people we want to question who would he capable of doing it, and whom we've had trouble with," he said.

Hayward said the Salt Lake County office was also working on a "number of leads" that developed since Miss Smith's body was found Oct. 27, more than a week after she disappeared from a restaurant.

The captain said he felt there had to be a connection between Miss Smith's death and the body found Wednesday.

"Basing my opinion on the type of wounds, the strangulation, the nature of the area where the bodies were found, the age of the victims and the rape, I would say there is a line."

He added, "We've got a real nut out there."

Debra Kent, daughter of Mr. and Mrs. Dean O. Kent, is still missing and reward money offered for information about her whereabouts has risen to $5,000. She was last seen by her parents Nov. 8 when she left a night play at Viewmont High School to meet her younger brother at a local skating rink.

Authorities are seeking any links between the kidnapping and attempted abductions.

December 2, 1974
Canyon Searchers Find No Traces
The Herald-Journal (Logan, Utah)

SALT LAKE CITY (UPI) - A weekend search of the canyons surrounding Salt Lake City produced no trace of two young women who mysteriously disappeared in recent weeks.

Authorities conducted the search on the theory the girls may have been kidnaped.

The bodies of two other teenage girls have been found in the Wasatch Mountains since Oct. 28. Both had been beaten, raped and strangled.

Members of the Salt Lake County Sheriff's Mounted Posse and Search and Rescue team covered Big and Little Cottonwood, Rose, Butterfield, Corner, Parley's and Millcreek canyons without finding a sign of 17-year-old Debra Kent of Bountiful of 16-year-old Nancy Wilcox of Salt Lake. Miss Kent disappeared Nov. 8, and authorities say Miss Wilcox has been missing about six weeks.

Hikers found the body of Laura Ann Aime, 17, Salem, last week in American Fork Canyon. The body of Melissa Smith, 17-year-old daughter of Midvale Police Chief Louis Smith, was found Oct. 28 near Summit Park in Parley's Canyon.

Authorities said the two killings were similar, and Sheriff's Capt. N.D. Hayward said "It is definite that the two appear to be linked together.

"We've got a real nut out there."

December 4, 1974
Murderous sex fiend stalking Utah?
Tacoma News Tribune (Tacoma, Washington)

SALT LAKE CITY (AP) - Fear appears to be spreading among women in Utah's most populous area in the wake of a recent series of suspected abductions and two known slayings, possibly by the same sex criminal.

Al least one other teenaged girl is believed to be an abduction victim, officers say, and a search of canyons along Utah's Wasatch Front was conducted during the weekend for bodies and other clues in the incidents.

The nude bodies of both slain girls were found in such canyons. Salt Lake County sheriff's Capt. Pete Hayward is among officers who, based on such things as types of wounds and the nature of the area where the bodies were found, believes there is a connection.

Hayward and police in suburban areas of Midvale, Murray and Bountiful say they are getting numerous calls from frightened women wanting protection.

"Many of them have asked me for permission to carry guns," reported Midvale Police Chief Louis S. Smith, whose own 17-year-old daughter Melissa was one of the two girls found raped, beaten and strangled within the past 14 months.

"They've called us at all times of the day and night and some of them have asked me personally to their homes, or they've come to my house. They're all frightened and this community is very concerned," he said Monday.

Murray Police Chief Calvin Gillen said he has sent detectives to lecture young women at schools on how they can protect themselves when alone.

"I'm sure they're scared," he said. "We see more house lights left on all night, and women are not out alone as much as they used to be. Some call us for advice and we readily give it to them," he said.

Hayward heads a two-county investigation into the death of Miss Smith, whose body was found Oct. 28. He said he is constantly asked to supply information for women wanting protection.

"There's a great deal of concern about these cases by more people than I've seen before," he said.

"People, not just the women, are walking more in groups; others who used to walk from one place to another either aren't going alone now or are going in groups; others tell us they have their families pick them up instead of going it by themselves."

While officers were investigating Miss Smith's death, the body of Laura Aime, 17, of Salem, Utah, was found last week.

Another 17-year-old, Debra Kent of Bountiful, disappeared Nov. 8, and authorities say she may have met with foul play. She was last seen attending a high school play with her parents, and officers discount the possibility of her being a runaway.

During the weekend, Salt Lake County officers said they were looking for Nancy Wilcox, 16, who has been missing for about six weeks.

"We hope and pray she's a runaway, but we can't take a chance," said Sheriff's Capt. John G. Nielsen Jr.

Denise Bellock, 28, told Salt Lake County officers last week she believes the man who stabbed her in her backyard also tried to abduct her the weekend before.

She said a man demanded she go with him in her car. She said she refused and "kneed the man in the groin," thus managing to free herself. Two days later, police said, the woman investigated barking dogs in her yard and was stabbed in the shoulder by a dark-complexioned man who walked away.

In Utah County, south of Salt Lake City, officers are working on at least nine reported rapes in the past two years. Last week, a Brigham Young University senior, Gerald W. Hicker, 23, Steilacoom, Wash., was bound over for trial in one of the cases.

Police said they had questioned him about an unsolved sex-related shooting death last March 11 of a woman he once dated, Barbara Jean Rocky. Her nude body was found in a canyon east of Salt Lake City, but no charges have been filed in that case.

The attempted abduction of a Murray girl less than two hours before Miss Kent disappeared lead officers to believe the incidents are related.

December 29, 1974
The Missing Girls...

At King County Police headquarters a detective pours through a mountain of tips about four girls reported missing during the year and the slaying of two others.

At present he has between 11,000 and 12,000 names to check out on his suspect list.

"Some of them are cranks," Det. Lt. Richard Kraske, who is in charge of the investigation, says. "A neighbor may get angry at another and set him up as a suspect. But the majority of calls and tips are from concerned citizens."

Four girls: Lynda Ann Healy, Donna Manson, Georgann Hawkins and Susan Rancourt, all in their late teens or early 20s are still missing. The bones of two, Denise Naslund and Janice Ott, were found in September near Issaquah.

The latter two disappeared from Lake Sammamish State Park on Sunday July 14. Witnesses described a suspect with the first name "Ted."

"The only way we'll come across 'Ted' is through identification by witnesses who were at Lake Sammamish that day," Lt. Kraske said, "They were pretty astute observers.

"It's a good possibility that 'Ted' has left the state. He'd be a fool to stay around here after all the publicity." Kraske has one detective on the case full time and another on the case part time.

"It's still on the active file and never will go into the inactive file as long as I'm here," he said.

Also unsolved at year's end is the disappearance from her home on Capitol Hill Feb. 21 of Heidi Peterson, 4. There have been widespread searches and international circulation of her picture.

January 1, 1975
'74 Bequeathed a List of 'Missing'

Vonnie:

It's been really nice knowing ya. We've had lots of fun on Thursdays (apparently a class). Have fun this summer and stay away from those better things in life.

← Lov,

Denise

The note in the 1970 Denny Junior High School yearbook to Vonnie Van Driel was penned in girlish script by Denise Naslund.

Both girls were 15 then. Four years later, both vanished without a trace, becoming parts of a chain of chilling, baffling disappearances of young women in 1974.

Sparse remains of Denise were found Sept. 7 in woods east of Issaquah, along with those of Janice Ott, 23. Both vanished from Lake Sammamish State Park July 14. A mysterious "Ted" has been widely sought in their disappearances. Mrs. Ott was seen in the park with him.

No trace has been found of Vonnie, who became Mrs. Todd Stuth last May 4. She vanished late Thanksgiving Eve from their home at 14215-24th Ave. S. as she was preparing dinner for her husband, due home from work at 1:15 a.m. from Pacific Car & Foundry in Renton. She left the television on, her purse with $150 in it, her cigarettes and personal effects in the house, taking only the clothes she wore and her coat.

Denise and Vonnie went through junior high together and most of high school at Sealth. But aside from being classmates, they weren't close social friends, their mothers say, and detectives see no connection in their disappearances.

The disappearances of Vonnie, Mrs. Ott and Ms. Naslund, as well as Heidi Peterson, 4, and four college co-eds constituted a baffling chain of "missings" for detectives in 1974.

Although the remains of Mrs. Ott and Ms. Naslund have been found. police, despite exhaustive searching and checking of endless leads, haven't taken anyone into custody in any of the cases.

The four missing co-eds:

Lynda Ann Healy, 21, Seattle, vanished from her basement bedroom in the University District Jan. 31.

Donna Gail Manson, 19, Auburn, who disappeared from Evergreen State College campus March 12.

Susan Rancourt, 18, Anchorage, who vanished from Central Washington State College campus, Ellensburg, April 17.

Georganne Hawkins, 18, Lakewood, who vanished from an alley behind her University of Washington sorority house June 11.

A Post-Intelligencer $5,000 reward, for information leading to the arrest and conviction of any person or persons responsible for the disappearances of the four above-named co-eds or of Held Peterson or Mrs. Ott or Ms. Naslund, remains in effect. The reward. posted bel the disappearance of Mrs. Stuth, does not include her.

The Thanksgiving Eve disappearance of Mrs. Stuth is about as baffling as the others.

But it has been learned that the missing Vonnie was talking to a sister on the phone about 11 o'clock that night. The sister, the last-known person to hear Vonnie's voice, said the telephone conversation was interrupted when a man came to the door of the Stuth residence.

Vonnie, returning to the phone, told her sister the man wanted to give the Stuths a dog - and asked Vonnie to come look at the animal, even though it was late at night. The sister quoted Vonnie as telling the man her husband would look at the dog next day. The man apparently left.

Everything appeared all right when they ended their phone conversation, and Vonnie was "excited" about getting the dog, the sister told Vonnie's mother.

About an hour later, when Stuth came home from work, his wife was missing.

But her coat was missing -- as if she'd hurriedly put it on to step outside briefly.

Lt. Richard Kraske of the King County sheriff's office yesterday confirmed to the P-I that county detectives sought to question a man in the case but "he wouldn't even discuss it - he knew his rights." The man had counsel from the public defender's office, said Kraske.

Kraske said police and Stuth, the missing woman's husband, conferred with the county prosecutor's office and were told evidence is lacking to charge anyone with any crime in the case.

Mrs. Kenneth Linstad, Vonnie's mother, says authorities told her they don't even have proof a crime has been committed, without additional evidence. Such evidence - also in the cases of the other missing women - could include discovery of a body.

Meanwhile, Todd Stuth, still living in his wifeless home and wondering about Vonnie's fate, returned to his job at the foundry yesterday after working with authorities and on his own in what appears a futile attempt to solve the mystery.

February 18, 1975
Body of missing nurse discovered.
The Daily Sentinel (Grand Junction, Colorado)

ASPEN, Colo. (AP) - The frozen body of a young woman, matching the description of a Michigan nurse missing for more than a month, was found near this Colorado ski resort.

The Pitkin County Sheriff's office said the body was found Monday, but no positive identification had been made because of the condition of the body.

Caryn Campbell, 23, a registered nurse from Dearborn, Mich., vanished Jan. 12 from a lodge at the Snowmass ski area where she and her fiancé, a Farmington, Mich., physician were staying.

The nude body was spotted along Owl Creek between Aspen and Snowmass by a passing motorist, Sheriff Carrol D. Whitmire said.

The body had been "chewed by animals" and appeared to have been moved from its original location "probably by animals," Whitmire said.

The body was taken to Denver General Hospital today for an autopsy and in hopes of making positive identification through dental charts, said Whitmire.

Miss Campbell, who arrived in Snowmass Jan. 11 with Dr. Raymond Gadowski, had purchased five days of ski lessons and skied on Jan. 12.

She went to dinner with Gadowski at a restaurant near the ski lodge where they were staying. When they returned to the lodge about 8:30 p.m., Miss Campbell told Gadowski she was going to her second-floor room to get a magazine, Whitmire said.

Miss Campbell was seen walking toward her room by other guests, Whitemire said, but she never returned.

March 5, 1975
Brenda Ball of Burien
Woman's Skull Identified

A human skull, found in a wooded area near North Bend Saturday, was identified through dental charts yesterday as that of Brenda Carol Ball, 22, who disappeared last June 1 from a South End tavern.

King County police said the identity of a second skull, found Monday some 150 feet from the remains of Brenda Ball, was not determined yesterday, but is expected today.

The medical examiner is still comparing the teeth in the skull with the dental X-ray charts of missing women, according to county homicide Capt. Nick Mackie.

Ms. Ball was last seen at 2 a.m. on June 1 at the Flame Tavern, 128th and Ambaum Road S. She asked a musician for a ride home, according to police.

He declined, and she was never seen again.

Capt. Mackie said that Denise Naslund, 18, was also known to have frequented the Flame Tavern.

Her remains, along with those of Janice Ott, 23, were found last September a short distance east of Issaquah on the north side of 1-90 near Lake Sammamish State Park, about 10 miles from the latest recovery site.

The remains of a third person were also found last fall. But Mackie said yesterday the identity of those bones will never be known "unless we come up with a suspect." All that was left of the third person was a thigh bone, a pelvis and a lumbar vertebra, he said.

Mackie said that the discovery of these skulls, without any clothing or jewelry in the area, is strengthening the assumption that sexual assault was involved in the deaths of the women and that they were dumped nude in the wooded area.

No clothing or jewelry was recovered near the remains of Ott or Naslund either, Mackie said. They were last seen at Lake Sammamish State Park July 14.

Although he had no evidence connecting the death-of Ms. Ball with the other two women, the captain said he hasn't "ruled out any connections."

County detectives are comparing soil samples found with the latest skulls with soil found with the remains of the two women last September to determine if they came from the same location.

A young man identified only as "Ted" has been sought in connection with the disappearance of Mrs. Ott and Ms. Naslund.

The man is believed to have approached several women at the park that day and was seen leaving the area with Ms. Ott. County police said Ms. Ball was last seen by her roommates in their apartment in the Burien area at 2 o'clock the afternoon before she disappeared.

Her roommates were leaving on a date, and she told them of plans to go to the Flame Tavern; according to police, Ms. Ball was known to have hitchhiked in the past, police said. She had talked of catching a ride to Sun Lakes State Park to meet friends on June 1, the day she disappeared.

Police said she was not reported missing until June 17.

Two Green River Community College students working on a forest survey project found the skull Identified as that of Ms. Ball Saturday afternoon in a brushy area about one-eighth mile from a powerline rood that runs east from Highway 18 in the Taylor Mountain area.

On Monday, the area was sealed off and a thorough search uncovered the second skull along with a jawbone belonging to Ms. Ball, about 160 feet from the first skull.

Searchers yesterday recovered more bone fragments, Mackie said. The captain said the search would resume today and would continue "as long as we're finding something."

About 75 young volunteers from the Explorer Search and Rescue organization worked with about 15 county policemen on the search yesterday.

Six other young women, ranging in age from 13 to 21, have vanished mysteriously In Seattle, King County and other parts of the state since January 1974. They are:

Lynda Ann Healy, 21, Seattle, who vanished from her bedroom in Seattle's University District Jan. 31.

Donna Gail Manson, 19, Auburn, 19, who disappeared from The Evergreen State College near Olympia March 12, 1974.

Susan Rancourt, 18, Anchorage, who vanished from the Central Washington State College campus in Ellensburg April 17.

Janna Marie Hanson, 13, of Mountlake Terrace, who has been missing since Dec. 28. Police there, however, have listed her as a runaway.

Georgeanne Hawkins, 18, Lakewood, who disappeared from an alley behind her University of Washington sorority house June 11.

Mrs. Vonnie Stuth, 19, who disappeared from her home at 14215-24th Ave. S. Thanksgiving Eve.

March 5, 1975

UW Co-ed's Remains Discovered

3rd Woman Also Identified

The remains of two more young women found in a search area near North Bend were Identified by King County police yesterday.

A jawbone found in the area yesterday was identified as that of Lynda Ann Healy, 21, a University of Washington senior and the first of eight young women to vanish from the Seattle area in 1974.

The remains of another body found earlier were identified last night as those of Roberta Kathleen Parks, 20, of Lafayatte, Calif., who was last seen on the campus of Oregon State University in Corvallis May 6 of last year.

Miss Healy disappeared from her University District rooming house Jan. 31, 1974.

The identifications yesterday were the second and third made from bones found at the site in the Taylor Mountain area.

King County police said the remains of four persons had now have been found at the site. A dentist in Anchorage, Alaska, yesterday worked toward identification of the remains of the fourth person.

Miss Parks was last seen at 11:05 p.m. on Monday, May 6, as she was leaving her residence hall at Oregon State University to go to the student union where she was to meet friends.

She was reported missing to the campus security office on Wednesday evening, May 8. No luggage had been taken, her bicycle was still at the residence hall, and she had no other known means of transportation, campus officials said.

A skull found Saturday was identified as that of Brenda Carol Ball, 2, last seen at a Burien tavern June 1.

Dale Rancourt of Anchorage, father of Susan Rancourt, 18, missing from Central Washington State College's campus at Ellensburg since April 17 told The Post-Intelligencer yesterday from Anchorage that he had been informed a second skull, found Monday, "tentatively" had been identified as that of his daughter. Rancourt said the "tentative" identification came to him from campus police, who, he said, had the information from King County police.

However, King County police, while agreeing they had sent X-ray films of the skull to Dr. Gerald M. Stranik, the Rancourts' dentist at Anchorage, said the Rancourt identification was "premature."

It was not clear last night whether the Parks identification had been made from the remains whose films were sent to Anchorage.

Police had said earlier that one skull might never be identified because there are no teeth. It also was unclear last night whether the unidentified remains were the skull with no teeth.

Miss Healy, daughter of Mr. and Mrs. James Healy of Bellevue, vanished from her bedroom in a rooming house at 5517 12th Ave. NE. She shared the house with four other UW co-eds.

Virtually the only clues to her disappearance were spots of Lynda's blood on her pillow and sheet. Her bed was found to be unusually well made the next morning - housemates said Lynda sometimes didn't make up her bed until later in the day.

The older home is in a poorly lit area of the University District. In addition, a door to the basement leads to the bedroom occupied by Ms. Healy.

Her father, James Healy, said he was informed by police who came to his Bellevue home yesterday. Healy said that while both he and Mrs. Healy had continued to hold out hope for Lynda, "things had looked pretty black the longer she remained missing."

He said he wants police to catch the murderer.

No clothes have been found known to have belonged to the women whose remains were discovered in the Taylor Mountain area, indicating the victims apparently were brought to the site nude.

This also was the case at a site just east of Issaquah, where sparse remains of Janice Ott, 23, and Denise Naslund, 19, were found last September. Both women vanished from Lake Sammamish State Park July 14 and a mysterious "Ted" - seen leaving the area with Ms. Ott - has been widely sought without results.

Is "Ted" a suspect in the other cases - including Ms. Healy's? Officers don't want to say but Susan Rancourt's father told the P.I: "I believe Ted took her."

He said he based his belief on the fact that a Ted-like person tried to entice two other Central Washington State College co-eds into his car on the campus by wearing an arm in a sling or cast and indicating he was having difficulty carrying books to the auto.

Campus police said yesterday the first incident occurred the night of April 14 (not April 21, as previously reported) and the other on April 17, the night Susan Rancourt vanished. The auto in both cases was a Volkswagen sedan, reported brown in one case and "yellowish" in the second.

The Ted at Lake Sammamish State Park also wore an arm in a sling or cast, drove a metallic brown Volkswagen sedan and asked women - including Ms. Ott - to help him put his sailboat atop his auto.

Still missing are Donna Gail Manson, 18, Auburn, who vanished from the Evergreen College campus March 12; Georganne Hawkins, 18, Lakewood, who disappeared from an alley behind her UW sorority house June 11, and Mrs. Vonnie

Stuth, 19, who vanished from her South End home Thanksgiving Eve.

Memorial services for Linda Ann Healy have been set for 2 p.m. Sunday at Eastgate Congregational Church, Bellevue.

March 8, 1975
Police Task Force on Co-ed Case
...New Hunt for Ted

The formation of a combined King County and Seattle police task force to tackle the case of the state's missing women was announced yesterday, as remains of a fourth body found on Taylor Mountain were identified as those of Susan Rancourt.

Miss Rancourt, 18, of Anchorage, has been missing from the Central Washington State College campus at Ellensburg since last April 17.

Capt. Nick Mackie said the task force, which will be in full operation next week, will involve eight men from both departments.

He said it would be starting from "the beginning" and would re-examine interviews with hundreds of young men who match the description of Ted", a prime suspect in at least some of the cases.

"The same method was used by Ted at least twice," Mackie said. "He disarmed the women by saying 'I am no threat, need help.'"

County police said the discovery of Miss Rancourt provides a "possible" link between the Taylor Mountain site and a wooded area 10 miles away where the bodies of Janice Ott, 23, and Denise Naslund, 19, were found last Sept. 17.

Both women vanished from Lake Sammamish State Park on July 14.

The mysterious, smooth-talking "Ted" was last seen accompanying Mrs. Ott out of the park July 14.

Mackie said a Ted-like person tried to entice a co-ed into his car on the Central Washington campus the same night that Susan Rancourt vanished.

He was wearing an arm in a sling or cast, and indicating he was having difficulty carrying books to his car, a Volkswagen Beetle sedan.

The Lake Sammamish "Ted" enlisted Mrs. Ott to help load a boat on his car, also a Volkswagen. He, too, was wearing his arm in a cast or sling.

The identification of Rancourt brings to four the number of women found on the wooded hillside near North Bend about four miles south of I-90. The other women are:

Lynda Ann Healy, 21, a University of Washington senior who vanished from her University District home Jan. 31, 1974.

Roberta Kathleen Parks, 29, Lafayette, Calif., who was last seen alive on the campus of Oregon State University in Corvallis May 6.

Brenda Carol Ball, 22, of Normandy Park, who disappeared from a Burien-area tavern June 1.

The identification of Miss Healy brought Seattle police into the investigation, which up until now has been primarily handled by the county police.

Capt. Mackie said that investigators believe the killer or killers at one time lived in the Issaquah area, because the women - who disappeared from various parts of Seattle and as far away as Corvallis, Ore. - were all brought to the wooded grave site.

Police are not sure where the bodies were actually left, Mackie said. In the case of Ott and Naslund, police found sites where the bodies had actually lain, he said.

"The pieces have been scattered all over the countryside," he said. "Most of them have been under leaves."

About 100 people have joined in the week-long, hands-and-knees search of the brushy hillside off Highway 18, the Auburn-Echo Lake cutoff between Issaquah and North Bend.

Searchers yesterday uncovered two pieces of jawbone, a few loose teeth and some light brown hair.

Mackie said that even with the latest discovery it appears that only four bodies are dumped at the site.

The search will continue through the weekend, he said.

The captain said the identification of the women was made through dental charts. Two skulls with upper teeth and two jawbones have been found. Police have refused to specify which jawbones and skulls belonged to which women.

"I'm not going to identify what belongs to what out of deference to the parents," Mackie said.

A third skullcap was also found at the Taylor Mountain site and the remains of another body were found with those of Ott and Naslund last September. Without teeth for comparison, those remains will never be identified, Mackie said.

From his home in Anchorage, Dale Rancourt, Susan's father, said the experience has "been like living a nightmare.

"Now, she has been found and that closes it," he said.

"As much as you hope, after you have carried this burden of not knowing for a year, even bad news can in this peculiar way be good news."

He said a scholarship fund in his daughter's name would be established at Central Washington State College.

March 9, 1975
Devil Cult Theory in Co-ed Deaths

The Seattle police officer looked at the missing women posters tacked on the wall of the homicide unit and shuddered.

"If this thing is ever solved," he said, "I think it is going to be so weird that it is going to blow everybody's mind."

There is a theory floating around the Public Safety Building among Seattle policemen that a ring of occult devil worshippers may be responsible for the disappearances and deaths of eight Washington and Oregon State women this past year.

As the theory goes, the occult fanatics have grabbed the women and ritualistically sacrificed them to some perverted god.

The women are chosen to type, goes the assumption, and it must be admitted that a glance at the missing posters gives the eerie impression that the women are sisters.

As strange as that theory sounds, it is no stranger than the facts of the case, which has become the biggest mystery of its kind in the state's history.

"You don't really think that something as bizarre can be true," mused County Police Capt. Nick Mackie.

Mackie is in charge of an eight-man combined task force of county and city police that has been formed to tackle the baffling case.

Mackie said the task force is going to start "from the beginning."

"Once you build up a theory, you're locked into it," observed county homicide Lt. Richard Kraske. "And along comes some surprise to knock it to pieces."

Two students from Green River Community College provided just such a surprise a week ago yesterday. It has led to the discovery of four of the state's missing women on a brush-covered area east of Highway 18 about four miles south of I-90.

The discovery has linked the deaths of the four with that of two others, a link resting only on the description of one man – the mysterious, smooth-talking "Ted."

"We are now faced with the possibility, and it is only a possibility, that the deaths of these women were caused by one man," Mackie said.

That possibility was strengthened by the accidental discovery of the two forestry students. They stumbled upon a skill, which was later identified as that of Brenda Carol Ball, 22, of Normandy Park, who was last seen at closing time June 1 in a South End Tavern.

Police say Ms. Ball asked a musician at the Flame Tavern, 128th and Ambaum Road S., for a ride home. He declined and she was not seen again that night.

Brenda's mother, Mrs. Rosemary Arnoud, of Kent, said that the parents of Brenda's roommate received a call from Brenda just before noon on the day she disappeared.

"Where was she, I'm wondering," Mrs. Arnoud said. "I'm thinking that if somebody took her from that tavern, they aren't talking."

County police say Ms. Ball was last seen by her roommates in their apartment in the Burien area at 2 o'clock the afternoon before she disappeared.

Her roommates were leaving on a date, and she told them of plans to go to the Flame Tavern, according to police.

Ms. Ball was known to have hitchhiked in the past, police said, and had talked of catching a ride to Sun Lakes State Park to meet friends on June 1, the day she vanished.

Because she liked to take off on trips, her disappearance was not reported until June 17.

The discovery of her skull last week triggered a massive search of the Taylor Mountain area, which turned up the skeletal remains of three other women:

Lynda Ann Healy, 21, a University of Washington senior with long brown hair and blue eyes, who vanished from her University District rooming house Jan. 31.

Robert Kathleen Parks, 20, of Lafayette, Calif., who also wore her hair long and straight, and was last seen on the campus of Oregon State University in Corvallis May 6.

Susan Elaine Rancourt, an 18-year-old with long blond hair and blue eyes, who vanished from the Central Washington State College campus in Ellensburg April 17.

The discovery of the four remains together has raised the strong presumption that all the Taylor Mountain victims were slain by the same person, or persons working together.

Thus, the Healy slaying is linked to the Ball, Parks and Rancourt slayings.

And the identification of Susan Rancourt has linked those four to the discovery of two women some 10 miles away last Sept. 17.

An early morning grouse hunter that morning stumbled on the remains of Janice Ott, 23, long, blond hair and blue eyes, and Denise Naslund, 18, long light brown hair and brown eyes.

Those remains were found a short distance east of Issaquah on the north side of I-90, near Lake Sammamish State Park.

Both women vanished from the crowded state recreation area on July 14.

There are no clues to Miss Naslund's disappearance. She was last seen in a rest room about 4 p.m. with an unknown woman in a bikini.

But Mrs. Ott was last seen with a man known only as "Ted," who witnesses say asked her to help him put his sailboat atop his brown Volkswagen sedan.

"Ted" is described as in his 20s, between 5 feet, 6 and 9 inches tall. He was of medium build, tanned and with blondish-brown hair that partly covered his ears.

Police say "Ted" approached at least five girls at the park that day. He was wearing his arm in a cast or sling and asked all of them to help him with the sailboat.

A man with a similar description was seen at the Central Washington State campus, according to police.

A young man with an arm in a sling approached two co-eds on the campus requesting help in carrying packages or books to his car.

The first reported encounter was on the night of April 14. The second was April 17, the night Miss Rancourt vanished.

Police say the April 14 encounter took place about 10 p.m. when a co-ed walking near the campus heard something fall to the ground behind her.

She told police she saw a man matching Ted's description struggling to carry some packages, with a sling causing him the trouble.

She offered to help carry the load. When they arrived at the car, he dropped his keys as he tried to unlock the passenger side door. They found the keys and she left, somewhat apprehensive.

On the day Susan Rancourt vanished, another co-ed told of meeting a young man, his arm in a sling, struggling to carry some books from his car to the library. She said she became frightened and walked away when he abruptly ordered her into his car.

At 9:30 p.m. the night of the 17th, Miss Rancourt, a freshman, was last seen as she started for her dorm across campus after attending a meeting in a hall four blocks away. She had left her laundry in a campus laundromat.

County police have also attempted to establish a tenuous link between "Ted" and the disappearance of Lynda Ann Healy.

She vanished from her bedroom in the basement of an older home in the University District the night of Jan. 31. Spots of blood were found on her pillow and sheet.

Mackie noted that witnesses at Lake Sammamish who encountered "Ted" say that he started at them a long time before approaching.

"It could be he had been watching her for quite a while," Mackie said.

The discovery of the four latest bodies still leaves the whereabouts of three other women a mystery:

Georgann Hawkins, 18, Lakewood, who disappeared from an alley behind her University of Washington sorority house June 11.

Donna Gail Manson, 19, Auburn, who disappeared from an alley behind her University of Washington sorority house June 11.

Mrs. Vonnie Stuth, 19, who disappeared from her home at 14215-24th Ave S. Thanksgiving Even.

A UW co-ed has provided a possible link between "Ted" and the disappearance of Miss Hawkins.

She said she helped an apparently disabled "Ted" look-alike cross the street just 30 minutes before Miss Hawkins vanished.

This "Ted" wobbled on crutches, instead of having his arm in a sling, and was carrying a briefcase which he kept dropping.

That incident occurred at NE 47th Street and 17th Avenue NE, less than two blocks from where Miss Hawkins disappeared.

Police have eliminated at least one known psychopath as a suspect in the multiple murders.

Identification of the four on Taylor Mountain has lifted suspicion from James Edward Ruzicka, 25, a convicted sexual psychopath who escaped from Western State Hospital the night Lynda Ann Healy disappeared.

Ruzicka was charged here last March 27 with the rape murders of two West Seattle girls in February 1974.

At the time he was charged, Ruzicka was in police custody in Beaverton, Ore., where he was charged last March 6 with the rape of a Beaverton girl. He has been convicted of that crime.

Police say Ruzicka was in jail when Ball, Rancourt and Parks disappeared.

In the case of Vonnie Stuth, Mackie said the prime suspect is Gary Addison Taylor, 38, from Michigan, who has been identified as the "phantom sniper" who in the past years attacked a number of women in that state. He has spent several years in mental institutions there.

Taylor lived in the same neighborhood as Mrs. Stuth and her husband. Since Mrs. Stuth's disappearance, Taylor has moved out of the state.

Mackie said that Taylor is not considered a very likely suspect in the other murders.

County police have interviewed hundreds of young men who fit "Ted's" description. They have examined hundreds of Volkswagens that match the suspect's metallic-colored bug.

One of the witnesses at Lake Sammamish was hypnotized twice in the hope that her subconscious would dredge up the VW license number, but with no success.

Mackie said the task force is going to start at "point zero." The detectives are going to re-examine every interview made with the "Ted" look-alikes.

The assumption is that the man involved in the deaths "very definitely" lives or "has lived in that south and east county area," Mackie said.

The county, with the help of several doctors, is preparing a voluminous psychiatric profile on "Ted."

Meanwhile, the search on Taylor Mountain will continue. To date, three skills, two jawbones, upper portions of a skull and a piece of skull crown have been found.

That discovery includes two pieces of jawbone, several loose teeth, bone fragments and light brown hair that are believed to be from the four identified women.

Yesterday more particles of bone and strands of hair were found on Taylor Mountain, as the search there continues.

As he looked at the smiling faces of the women staring down from a composite poster the county had drawn up, Mackie had a few words of advice for Puget Sound area women.

"The man always uses the same method," Mackie said. "He operates with a sling and gets their sympathy.

"He's disarming them (his victims) by saying 'I'm no threat. I need help.'"

Turn the request down, Mackie advised.

"And the next thing they should do, and I hope people will do it, is to notify us."

March 16, 1975
Search for Slayer of 6 Young Women Is Frustrating

The county-city police task force's massive search for the slayer or slayers of six young women from this area is full of frustrations.

(Three other young women remain missing after remains of the six have been identified).

The foremost frustration:

A public anxious to help police catch the elusive "Ted," the chief suspect, has been flooding the taskforce with "sightings" of him.

But virtually all detail Ted as he looked last July 14, when seen at Lake Sammamish State Park near Issaquah. Janice Ott, 23, and Denise Naslund, 19, vanished from the park that day. Ms. Ott was seen leaving with Ted. Remains of both women were found near Issaquah last September.

Police agree that Ted - unless he is grossly careless or downright dumb or WANTS to be caught - could look entirely different now than he did July 14.

If he has changed his appearance substantially, and odds are he has, Ted could be sitting across the table from you and you wouldn't recognize him," an officer said.

His description, after Lake Sammamish, was a man in his 20s, between 5 feet 6 inches and 5 feet 8 inches tall, about 160 to 170 pounds, medium build, tanned, blonde-brown hair long enough to cover the ears and longer in back. He had his left arm in a sling or cast, his manner was very pleasant, and he smiled a lot. He drove a brown Volkswagen beetle.

But King County Detective Capt. Nick Mackie, heading the task force, agrees that Ted today could have, for example, a crewcut dyed black; no sling or cast on arms, could be driving-a big station wagon — and have changed his manner completely.

Or Ted could have been in disguise, wig, etc., at the park.

Yet, reports continue pouring in on suspects looking like Ted did last July. Several published composites, depicting Ted as he looked then, ironically could be misleading if the man now looks different. The reports would be of no help and could be a hindrance.

This fact caused Mackie to say so, in a nice way, this week. Most of the new reports, he said, weren't of much help. Instead, he appealed to persons who know Ted to contact police. He even asked Ted to turn himself in and get psychiatric help.

Another frustration:

Even if Ted hasn't altered his appearance, he may never have been seen in this area, because he may have left, possibly shortly after July 14. No similar disappearances of co-eds or women in that age group that fit the pattern of the earlier disappearance have been reported. (Mrs. Vonnie Stuth of Burien vanished last Thanksgiving eve, but police are hunting another suspect. A Mountlake Terrace teenager also is missing but police of that city think she's a runaway.)

A third frustration faced by the task force:

Roberta Kathleen Parks, 19, a co-ed, vanished last May 6 from the Oregon State University campus at Corvallis; her sparse remains were found last week at Taylor Mountain near North Bend. When she left her OSU dorm that night, she told girlfriends she was going after something to eat.

If Ms. Parks were abducted on or near the OSU campus, as some believe, why would the kidnaper risk taking her almost 250 miles – and across a state line – to bring her up to this area? Was Ms. Parks dead or alive when she was taken across the Washington-Oregon border?

But the Federal Bureau of Investigation hasn't entered the case. The FBI's national resources would add considerable muscle to the local task force's efforts.

Why hasn't the FBI come in?

"Because there is no indication of a violation of the federal kidnaping statute, which is the only way we could enter the case," explained an FBI spokesman here yesterday.

"Nobody (except maybe Ted) knows how Ms. Parks got to this area. You can't say he picked her up down there and brought her across the border to kill her…"

The OSU co-ed was known to hitchhike sometimes.

Forced abduction, a ransom-demand and transport in interstate commerce.

Authorities don't know Ms. Parks was abducted in Oregon, and there have been no ransom demands on any of the missing women. Whether Ms. Parks was taken across the state line or crossed of-her own volition isn't known.

However, the FBI has offered its lab and identification facilities to the local task force and will help check out-of-state leads.

Mackie's appeal to Ted to turn himself in may not be as desperate a move as it might seem. Could Ted - like some psychopaths, firebugs and others - deep down actually want to get caught?

The possibility can't be discarded, although it's a long shot. Mackie says:

"If he wanted to be caught, he may have been purposefully risking it at Lake Sammamish last July. Remember, all the previous single disappearances occurred at night.

"But at Sammamish, Ted came out into the daylights. And two women vanished from the park that day. We know Ted struck out with at least five other women there before Ms. Ott went with him. More may have seen him and not reported it to us." (Two co-eds saw a Ted-like person at Central Washington State College in April, one the same night Susan Rancourt, 18, vanished from the Ellensburg campus.)

The composite pictures of Ted were based on the above descriptions. The difficulty is that the composites resemble many other young men with similar features and haircuts.

And while Ted smiled at a lot of people, the composite showed a rather grim-looking man.

March 26, 1975
1,200 Names in 'Ted' Suspect File

The names of over 1,200 individuals are on file with the county-city homicide task force as possible suspects in the case of the missing women, police said yesterday.

Capt. Nick Mackie said that a "couple hundred really warrant digging into until we've definitely established that the person isn't the suspect."

The task force was formed when the skeletal remains of four women were found in the Taylor Mountain area near North Bend earlier this month. The bones of two other identified remains of a third person were found last September near Issaquah.

Police are searching for a man known only as "Ted," who was last seen the day two women vanished from Lake Sammamish State Park July 14.

Mackie also stated that the 11-man unit has leads on 600 vehicles, including Volkswagens - the type of car "Ted" may have been driving at Lake Sammamish. The captain said calls are still coming in from citizens who say they have seen the suspect. All the tips are being prioritized, he said.

"They are being ranked as to value, not where they came from," Mackie said. "Leads that come from me or Sheriff Larry Waldt are not getting special attention."

Mackie expressed the general frustration that has plagued the investigation from the beginning.

Nearly 10 people saw or heard "Ted" at Lake Sammamish that hot July day. Over 40,000 people attended the park the day the women vanished, and the County has pored over hundreds of snapshots and movies taken that day.

The police also enlarged pictures taken in the parking lot, looking for license numbers on Volkswagens. All in vain.

"Sometimes, I just can't believe we didn't come up with a picture of the guy that day," mused Mackie. "It just boggles the mind."

He said that if a picture had identified the suspect, police at the time would not have been able to hold the man in custody.

"We had no bodies, and therefore, no crime," he said.

The remains of Janice Ott and Denise Naslund, who disappeared from the state park the same day, were found three months later on a wooded hillside near Issaquah.

As for "progress" in the case, Mackie said he would only discuss the term 'when the police have somebody in jail.

"When we file charges," he said. "That's when there will be some progress."

March 27, 1975
Women's Bones - A Grim Theory

The grim possibility arose yesterday that four young women whose sparse remains were found in the North Bend area early this month were decapitated, according to the King County medical examiner's office.

"It would fit the facts," an official in the officer told the Post-Intelligencer. He asked that his name not be used.

Only "skull and lower jawbones of the four were found at the Taylor Mountain site, the official said, with other bones identified as animal. About 18 bags of bones were recovered from the site and the official said that so far as he knows the examiner's officer has seen them all.

He said authorities are puzzled on why no other type of human bones have turned up. Asked if this could indicate decapitation, the official responded:

"It is plausible and would explain the failure to find any other type of human bones. It would be reasonable to expect to find other remains if they had been left there along with the heads."

The official said this also would explain why no clothes worn by the missing women were found there.

There is some possibility that animals had carried away all body bones but not the skulls, the examiner's official went on. Yet, thorough screening of the area for bones failed to turn up any other identifiable human remains and this is surprising, the official said.

When remains of three persons, including Denise Naslund, 19, Janice Ott, 23, were found near Issaquah last September, the bones included both skull and body parts.

Both women vanished from Lake Sammamish State Park July 14. A mysterious "Ted" has been widely sought in the disappearances.

Skulls and lower jawbones found at the Taylor Mountain site this month resulted in identification of Lynda Ann Healy, 21, missing from the University District since Jan. 31, 1974; Susan Elaine Rancourt, 18, who vanished from Central Washington State College campus at Ellensburg last April 17; Roberta Kathleen Parks, 20, missing from Oregon State University Campus, Corvallis, since last May 6 and Brenda Ball, 22, missing from the Burien area since last June 1.

The third person whose remains were found near Issaquah never has been identified. A skullcap found at the Taylor Mountain site also hasn't been identified, although it could belong to one of the two jawbones found there.

Three other young women are still missing. They are Donna Gail Manson, 19, who vanished from The Evergreen State College near Olympia March 12, 1974; Georgann Hawkins, 18, who disappeared from the University District June 11, Mrs. Vonnie Stuth, who vanished from her South End home last Thanksgiving Eve.

King County Sheriff Lawrence Waldt -said he had "no comment at this time" on the decapitation report.

"I anticipate a news release Thursday (today) on the case, possibly with new information," he said, but declined to say if the news release involved the decapitation possibility.

March 28, 1975
Police Confirm Only Skulls Were Found

County police confirmed yesterday a report first published in The Post-Intelligencer that the only human remains found in a 4-million square foot search of Taylor Mountain were the skills and jawbones of four missing women.

Capt. Nick Mackie refused comment on speculation the women were decapitated. But he did say police were "very perplexed" that no other human bones had been found.

Mackie also revealed that along with the remains of three people found at Issaquah last September, several gunny sacks filled with young immature elk carcasses were found some 300 feet from the human remains.

A spokesman for the State Game Department said that elk are "still a rarity" in the Issaquah-North Bend area. He said "poachers" could have been responsible for dumping the sacks on the wooded hillside.

A veterinarian had initially identified the bones in the sacks as those of goats – animals favored since ancient times for symbolic sacrificial rites. The initial reports gave rise to the theory that a "devil cult" could be responsible for the slayings.

Regarding the Taylor Mountain discovery, a source in the King County Medical Examiner's office told the P-I Wednesday that the decapitation theory "would fit the facts" of the case.

County police are reluctant to theorize about how the women died. "We just don't want to when we don't have the facts," Mackie said.

But it is admitted that the possible decapitation of the women is being considered. And the captain could offer no explanation as to why only human skills and lower jawbones were found in the massive, hands-and-knees search that lasted over a week earlier this month.

"I'm as amazed as anyone else is," Mackie said.

The anthropology department at the University of Washington determined that the only human bones discovered were skulls and lower jawbones.

The 13,000-man hour search recovered some 156 specimens, Mackie said. The county retained 92 for analysis, and 40 to 45 were determined to be bone fragments, he said.

Except for the skulls and jaw bones, none of those remains were human. Mackie said the rest were predominantly deer remains and a few cow bones.

When skeletal remains of three persons, including Denise Naslund, 19, and Janice Ott, 23, were found near Issaquah last September, the bones included both skull and body parts.

Both women vanished from Lake Sammamish State Park July 14. A mysterious "Ted" has been widely sought in the disappearances.

"The bodies at Issaquah were in one piece for a long period of time," Mackie said. "I can't say that for a fact at Taylor Mountain."

County police have long held to the assumption that animals had carried away all body bones, but not the skulls.

However, Mackie said yesterday that "one would think" that at least a few other human remains would have been found along with the skulls.

He did say that the soil was different at Taylor Mountain than at the Issaquah site - more wet, boggy and swampy - and that the other bones "could" have decomposed more quickly.

The decapitation theory will be discussed with a local psychiatrist, who is preparing a psychological profile of "Ted", the prime suspect in the slayings.

"If we are dealing with a sexual psychopath," Mackie stated, "the fact of decapitation or not decapitation really wouldn't have a hearing on the type of person we're looking for."

Mackie said that the latest count showed that the names of 1,912 possible "Ted" suspects were on file with the county-city task force tackling the case.

He said the unit has eliminated "all but 200" of those names for further investigation.

The captain also noted that the task force has descriptions of 824 vehicles including Volkswagens – the type of car "Ted" may have been driving at Lake Sammamish.

Skulls and lower jaw bones found at the Taylor Mountain site resulted in identification of Lynda Ann Healy, 21, missing from the University District since Jan. 31, 1974; Susan Elaine Rancourt, 18, who vanished from Central Washington State College campus at Ellensburg last April 17; Roberta Kathleen Parks, 20, missing from Oregon State University campus, Corvallis, since last May 6 and Brenda Ball, 22, missing from the Burien area since last June 1.

Three other young women are still missing. They are Donna Gail Manson, 19, who vanished from the Evergreen State College near Olympia March 12; Georgann Hawkins, 18, who disappeared from the University District June 11, and Mrs. Vonnie Stuth, who vanished from her South End home last Thanksgiving Eve.

April 11, 1975
Colorado Bureau of Investigation - Special Bulletin
MISSING PERSON

JULIE CUNNINGHAM, W/F, Age 26, 5'5", 110 lbs., long dark brown hair (parted down the middle), brown eyes (does not wear glasses), has pierced ears, right-handed, DOB 1-10-49.

Miss Cunningham was last seen in Vail, Colorado at her apartment complex at approximately 6:30 p.m. on March 18, 1975. She is believed to be wearing a brown suede jacket with sheepskin lining, blue jeans, mid-calf brown leather boots, and either a brown or white ski hat.

Miss Cunningham was last seen on foot and left all her personal belongings and vehicle behind.

Refer any information to: Chief Gary R. Wall, Vail Police Department.

April 24, 1975
'Zodiac' Ruled Out As Savage 'Ted'

King County police yesterday dismissed a California police theory that eight Northwest women were killed by a single man also responsible for the deaths of nearly 40 other women in four other Western states.

The San Francisco Examiner published a report yesterday that Sonoma County Sheriff Don Streipeke believes a man known as the "Zodiac" killer is responsible for the deaths of some six women found in the mountains east of Seattle last month.

The same man, Striepeke said, is responsible for the deaths of some 28 northern California girls and women, ages 12 to 24.

King County Police Capt. Nick Mackie said his office has consulted with Sonoma County Sgt. Erwin Carlstedt "and reached the conclusion that there was no connection."

Last month Carlstedt attended a meeting in Seattle of authorities from Canada to California.

"We came to the definite conclusion that there was no relationship between his murders and our murders," Mackie declared.

Carlstedt, the investigator who developed the mass-murder theory for the sheriff, could not be reached for comment. He was traveling between Utah and Colorado.

A spokesman for Sheriff Streipeke did not discount the Examiner's report, but angrily declared that it did not come "from an official press release."

The sheriff has called nearly 50 Northern California newsmen to a news conference tomorrow to outline the bizarre mass-murder theory.

Sonoma Undersheriff John Hess said there "may be a connection" between the California and Washington slayings, but would not elaborate.

Carlstedt is quoted as saying that the prime suspect is a man known only as the "Zodiac," who has claimed up to 37 murders in the San Francisco Bay area. Police there have accounted him responsible for six.

Carlstedt said that a psychological profile of "Ted," the prime suspect in the Washington slayings, "overlaps" with a profile done on the Zodiac killer.

"There is no doubt in my mind," Carlstedt said, "that the same man killed the young women in Washington State."

Mackie, in dismissing the sergeant's speculations, noted that King County doesn't even have a psychological profile of "Ted." They don't have enough evidence to create one, he added.

"Their suspect doesn't fit our 'Ted' description at all," Mackie said.

The captain said that Carlstedt "made some mention" of the Zodiac killer on his visit to Seattle, "but there was never any indication whatsoever that we are working on the same type of case."

Mackie explained that the Sonoma County murders involved hitchhikers, girls selected at random. In contrast, Mackie said, "Ted" used the ruse of a disabled arm to entice specific girls away from safety.

He said most of the missing women here were college students, except for the two women who disappeared July 14 from Lake Sammamish State Park. The women in California were much younger, he said.

"If they feel there is definitely a connection between their murders and ours," Mackie concluded, "then they have some information they haven't given to us."

Undersheriff Hess admitted that the theory was "speculation," but argued that there was no evidence to prove it false. He also admitted, however, that there was no specific evidence to prove it true.

In explaining their theory, Carlstedt and Striepeke said a symbol from ancient English witchcraft was found near a remote site in California where the bodies of three young women were found.

The symbol was two rectangles connected by a line, formed by twigs, with two stones lying inside one of the rectangles.

Striepeke said the symbol once was put on the hearth of homes of the dead in England to "speed the deceased to the afterlife." He said the Zodiac killer had written of his intended random victims as "slaves I will collect for my afterlife."

Mackie noted there was no such symbol found along with the women's skeletal remains discovered at Issaquah and Taylor Mountain sites.

Carlstedt believes the killer may be leaving a trail of bodies over several Western states that traces the letter "Z" running from San Francisco to Seattle, then crossing down through Salt Lake City to Vail, Colo. He said if the theory is correct, the killer's trail will move north from Vail.

Homicide inspectors in San Francisco were not prepared to accept the theory of a lone killer.

In King County, detectives reacted with disbelieve to the published reports. "I can't believe that Carlstedt even said that," one detective commented.

May 12, 1975
Idaho State Journal (Pocatello, Idaho)

LYNETTE CULVER, 12-year-old daughter of Mr. and Mrs. Edward A. Culver, 231 Fairbanks, has been missing since last Tuesday after being seen at Alameda Junior High School. According to Pocatello police, the girl is five feet two inches tall, has blue eyes and long brown hair, and weighs about 105 pounds. When last seen, she was wearing blue jeans and red checkered shirt with a maroon, fur-collared jacket. Persons having information about Lynette's whereabouts are asked to contact the Pocatello Police Department.

May 27, 1975
Enumclaw Body That Of Vonnie Stuth

King County officials yesterday positively identified through dental records the body of Mrs. Vonnie Stuth, 18, who was found in a shallow grave near Enumclaw Saturday.

Cause of death was a gunshot wound to the bead, according to deputy chief medical examiner Donald T. Reay.

The Burien housewife had been dead about six months, Reay said, which would coincide with the time of her disappearance last Thanksgiving eve.

The decomposition of the body made it impossible to determine if she was sexually abused or otherwise assaulted, Reah said.

Mrs. Stuth's body was found behind the Enumclaw-area house of one-time mental patient Gary Addison Taylor, 39, who is the principal suspect in her disappearance. Taylor lived in the house at 40224-228th Way SE. northwest of Enumclaw, at the time Mrs. Stuth vanished.

Taylor is being held in Houston, Tex. on charges of rape, attempted rape, and sexual abuse involving attacks on four women and a 17-year-old Houston girl. Bail has been set at $140.000.

County Police Capt. Nick Mackie said yesterday that authorities there have placed a "hold" on Taylor, meaning that even if he manages to post bond, he will not be released from the Houston jail.

Mackie said the King County Prosecutor's office is in "no hurry" to file charges against Taylor. "The more information we have, the better off we are," Mackie said.

The prosecutor, however, is "extremely worried about pre-trial publicity," Mackie said.

"We have to be very careful," Mackie said. "We can't divulge the details of our investigation. All the releases have been coming from other parts of the country."

A King County detective is being sent to Houston to question Taylor, Mackie said. Although no immediate plans for extradition have been made, the captain said, "when our turn comes, we will want him."

In Michigan, Lenawee County Sheriff Richard Germond said Taylor is under suspicion in the murder of two women, whose bodies were found earlier this month behind a house he had once lived in.

Like Mrs. Stuth, the women had been shot in the head.

In addition, Taylor is wanted by Colorado authorities for questioning in connection with the murders earlier this year of two young women in Aspen and Vail, Colo.

Taylor spent 13 years in Michigan mental institutions until he was placed on convalescent leave in 1971. He dropped out of the outpatient program in 1973 and was officially listed as an escapee last November.

The discovery of Mrs. Stuth still leaves county police with the unsolved murders of at least six other young women.

A massive search in March in the Taylor Mountain area uncovered the remains of Lynda Ann Healy, 21; Susan Elaine Rancourt, 18; Brenda Ball, 22, and Roberta Kathleen Parks, 20. The remains of Denise Naslund, 18, and Janice Ott, 23, were discovered last September near Issaquah. Two women still listed as missing are Donna Manson, 16, and Georgann Hawkins, 18.

An 11-man task force handling the case is searching for a man known only as "Ted," who was last seen when Ott and Naslund vanished from Lake Sammamish State Park July 14.

Mackie said Taylor's picture has been shown to witnesses who were at the park that day and they have concurred that Taylor "definitely is not 'Ted.'"

But county police have no hard and fast evidence that "Ted" is the man they are looking for.

The strongest piece of evidence is the sighting by two women of a man matching "Ted's" description at Central Washington

State College in Ellensburg the night Susan Rancourt disappeared.

As at Lake Sammamish, this suspect carried his arm in a sling, using the apparent disability to entice women from safety and drove a Volkswagen.

"This is what we haven't been able to explain," Mackie said yesterday. "Ted is our suspect because he used the ruse of the sling in both places and drove Volkswagens."

June 1, 1975
County Cuts 'Ted' Task Force Down to 2 Men

King County police have trimmed the "Ted" task force to two detectives after exhausting the bulk of more than 2,500 leads available to them since the case of the state's missing and murdered women began to develop last July.

Nine of the 11 county and Seattle police detectives tackling the case packed their bags Friday and returned to regular duties.

Their work is all but finished, police say. And although the manhunt failed to pinpoint the murderer responsible for the deaths of at least nine young women last year, it went a long way in proving who he isn't.

The detectives spent the better part of the last 12 weeks crowded into a small, L-shaped room in the King County Courthouse.

In that room, the smiling faces of the missing women stare down from police posters tacked on the walls, constant reminders of the task at hand.

A large diagram of Lake Sammamish State Park is propped up on one of the desks. It tracks the elusive movements last July 14 of a man known only as "Ted," the prime suspect in the disappearances.

On that day two women - one of whom last was seen leaving with the mysterious stranger - vanished without a trace.

That same man talked to 10 other people that day, and their names are penciled in on the white storyboard, marks indicating where contact was made.

The names and addresses of those witnesses represent the county's most important clue.

"In most homicides, the killer leaves a bit of himself at the scene and takes a bit of the scene away with him," explained Capt. Nick Mackie, in charge of the Task Force.

"In this case, the only evidence we have is the suspect's presence."

Two five-foot filing cabinets dominates a third of the narrow office, metallic green drawers bulging with mountains of other evidence collected in this, the state's biggest murder mystery.

The Task Force was formed March 7, in the wake of the grisly discovery of the skeletal remains of four women in a wooded swamp on Taylor Mountain in North Bend.

The unit's initial task was to start from "point zero," to re-examine the interviews with hundreds of young men who were "Ted" look-alikes.

Mackie said then that the chances were "very slight" that previous investigators had overlooked anything. But doubts remained, Mackie confessed, doubts he wanted laid to rest.

Searchers at Taylor Mountain found the remains of Brenda Ball, 22; Lynda Ann Healy, 21; Susan Elaine Rancourt, 18, and Roberta Kathleen Parks, 20.

Police feel there is a link between the Taylor Mountain slayings and those of Janice Ott, 23, and Denise Naslund, 19, whose remains were found in a wooded area near Issaquah last Sept. 17. The remains of a third person were also found then, but authorities have been unable to provide any identification.

Still missing are Donna Gail Manson, 19, from The Evergreen State College near Olympia, and Georganne Hawkins, 18, who vanished from the University of Washington.

The Task Force was not able to being its labor immediately.

With the massive publicity surrounding the case, phantom "Teds" began cropping up in the minds of citizens everywhere – at supermarkets, drive-ins, bowling alleys and golf courses. The detectives were swamped with a flood of new "leads" on their suspect's whereabouts, as many as 300 a day.

"The information was coming in so fast and heavy that we were just stockpiling it," said a frustrated Mackie.

Over 2,550 leads on possible "Teds" had been received at last count, as well as sightings of hundreds of vehicles, including Volkswagens, the type of car "Ted" may have driven.

Each tip was assigned to a detective, who put the name or circumstance on a filing card. That card was cross-filed and checked to determine that work was not being duplicated.

If the tip was a sighting and the witness had managed to get an address, a name or a license number, police obtained a picture of the suspect - by a method they would rather not divulge - and compared it with the color-composite picture of "Ted."

This method eliminated many of the more superficial leads.

Not relying solely on the composite picture ("I don't trust them anyway," Mackie has said), detectives hit the street to interview friends, relatives and the suspects themselves.

One man whom police have taken a hard look at is Gary Addison Taylor, who has been charged in connection with the death of Mrs. Vonnie Stuth, 18, a Burien housewife whose body was discovered recently near an Enumclaw home where Taylor used to live.

Taylor's picture has been shown to the sharp-eyed Lake Sammamish witnesses. They concur: Taylor definitely is not "Ted."

Although police have no hard and fast evidence that "Ted" is their man, there is one coincidence that points this way:

Two women sighted a man matching "Ted's" description at Central Washington State College in Ellensburg the night Susan Rancourt disappeared.

As at Lake Sammamish, this suspect carried his arm in a sling, using the apparent disability to entice women. And he drove a Volkswagen.

"That is what we haven't been able to explain," Mackie said. "Ted is our suspect because he used the ruse of the sling in both places and drove a Volkswagens."

The Task Force members also took another look at the photographs taken by amateur shutterbugs that hot July day at the state park. The county offered to develop the film free if the public would only turn in their photos.

In the hundreds of pictures and home movies taken by the 40,000 people at the beach that day, there was only one picture of man with his arm in a sling or cast, and he was playing volleyball.

As a last gasp attempt to catch the elusive killer, police have turned to technology. Computer operators are presently key-punching reams of data, collecting information on friends, classmates and acquaintances of the woman, all "Ted" suspects VW owners into one gigantic computer run.

Also being fed into that computer are the names of some 1,900 convicted sexual psychopaths, all of whom had spent time at Western State Hospital and were outside the walls the day Denise Naslund and Janice Ott disappeared. What has made the search so maddening is that police haven't a clue as to how the women died. Nor do they have a personality profile of their suspect. Local doctors were drafted to create a "psychological profile" of the Lake Sammamish murderer, but the effort proved fruitless.

June 24, 1975
Police look for missing woman
The Daily Sentinel (Grand Junction, Colorado)

A 24-year-old Grand Junction woman missing since April 6 has become the focus of an intensive investigation by city police.

Police report no leads in the disappearance of Denise Lynn Oliverson, of 1619 LaVeta, who was last seen riding a bicycle from her residence at 3 p.m. April 6.

Mr. and Mrs. Robert D. Nicholson, of 801 Ouray, reported her missing April 7 after a friend of the woman said she had been on her way to Lincoln Park.

On that day police found Mrs. Oliverson's bicycle and shoes under the Fifth Street bridge near railroad tracks but have been unable to come up with any leads since.

Capt. Robert Burnett said today the Colorado Bureau of Investigation was asked to provide assistance this month in distributing information concerning her disappearance to police agencies through the western state area.

He said a number of interviews with friends and relatives of Mrs. Oliverson have failed to turn up any clues.

According to her father, she had planned to stop at her parents' home before or after a trip to Lincoln Park. He could give no reason for her disappearance,

Nicholson said he contacted the Federal Bureau of Investigation for assistance after she was reported missing, however, was told they will not become involved unless there is indication of death resulting from foul play, kidnapping or extortion.

According to the CBI bulletin she is described as 5'4" tall, with long brown hair and blue eyes. She was last seen wearing blue jeans and an Indian print blouse.

Mrs. Oliverson was graduated from Grand Junction High School in 1968. She was employed at Dixson Inc. as an assembler in 1974.

She was divorced following a short marriage in 1972.

Persons with information concerning her disappearance are asked to contact the police.

July 4, 1975
Police Ask Help Locating a Girl
The Daily Herald (Provo, Utah)

Security police at Brigham Young University and Provo police have requested public help in their search for a 13-year-old North Salt Lake girl who has been missing for a week.

BYU Security Chief Robert W Kelshaw explained the girl, named Susan Curtis, arrived at BYU last Friday for a youth conference and has been missing since then except for one occasion this past Tuesday when she was observed briefly at the rear of one professor's class trying to sell a textbook, according to the professor who definitely identified her from her picture.

Chief Kelshaw reported the girl stands 5 feet 7, weighs about 120 pounds, has light brown hair and hazel eyes. He said she was wearing a full-length evening dress when she first turned up missing last Friday. But on Tuesday, when observed by the professor, he said she was wearing a blue knit top and faded blue jeans.

A security policeman also noted that she now wears braces on her teeth.

Chief Kelshaw reported that on previous occasions she has disappeared or run away for a number of days at a time and for that reason, plus the identification by the professor, he does not believe there has been any abduction.

The chief added that anyone having any information as to her whereabouts should contact either BYU Security or notify Provo police.

July 12, 1975
Probe Continues In 'Ted' Cases

On the eve of the first anniversary of the biggest manhunt in the state's history, King County police said yesterday they are still optimistic that the case of the state's missing and murdered women will be solved.

Denise Naslund and Janice Ott vanished from Lake Sammamish State Park last July 14. Their remains, along with those of four other women, have been found in the mountains east of Seattle.

Capt. Nick Mackle said a massive computer run involving 14,000 names has turned up some "interesting coincidences" that detectives are examining to determine if they are "hard leads."

Into that computer were fed the names of sexual psychopaths, "Ted" suspects, acquaintances and classmates of the missing women.

Detectives have eliminated some 2,684 "Ted" suspects and have investigated over 1,000 suspect vehicles. Three persons, including a woman detective from the morals unit, are still assigned fulltime to the case.

"I'm still optimistic," Mackie said. However, the county's big "break," Mackie fearfully admitted, could come if the killer strikes again and this time makes a mistake.

"I have been fearful that this could be the way we crack the case," Mackie said. If a suspect were found, it would be a "very easy investigation," he said.

Because the girls disappeared from such distant points as Seattle, Ellensburg and Corvallis, Ore., detectives would be able to correlate a suspect's movements with the disappearances, the captain explained.

"Unfortunately, we don't have a prime suspect," Mackie concluded. "But we are not slacking off. And I am confident that the county's biggest, baffling and most bizarre case will be solved."

August 16, 1975

Theodore Robert Bundy, a law student at the University of Utah, was arrested by Utah Highway Patrol officer Bob Hayward in Granger, a Salt Lake City suburb, after Hayward observed Bundy cruising a residential area in his Volkswagen Beetle during the pre-dawn hours and fleeing at high speed after seeing the patrol car. Hayward noticed that the Volkswagen's front passenger seat had been removed and placed on the rear seats and searched the car. He found a ski mask, a second mask fashioned from pantyhose, a crowbar, handcuffs, trash bags, a coil of rope, an ice pick, and other items initially assumed to be burglary tools. Bundy explained that the ski mask was for skiing, he had found the handcuffs in a dumpster, and the rest were common household items.

In a search of Bundy's apartment, police found a guide to Colorado ski resorts with a checkmark by the Wildwood Inn, and a brochure that advertised the Viewmont High School play in Bountiful, where Debra Kent had disappeared. Lacking sufficient evidence to detain Bundy, he was released on his own recognizance.

Salt Lake City police placed Bundy on 24-hour surveillance.

The house Lynda Ann Healy was abducted from at 5517 12th Ave.

Lynda Ann Healy's room as investigators found it.

Georgann Hawkins

The alley along Greek Row at the University of Washington where Georgann was abducted.

The missing co-eds from the Pacific Northwest

Janice Ott (top) and Denise Naslund (below) both disappeared from Lake Sammamish State Park on the same day.

Investigators initially focused on Janice Ott's missing bike. Below, an aerial view of Lake Sammamish State Park and the approximate locations Ott and Naslund were last seen.

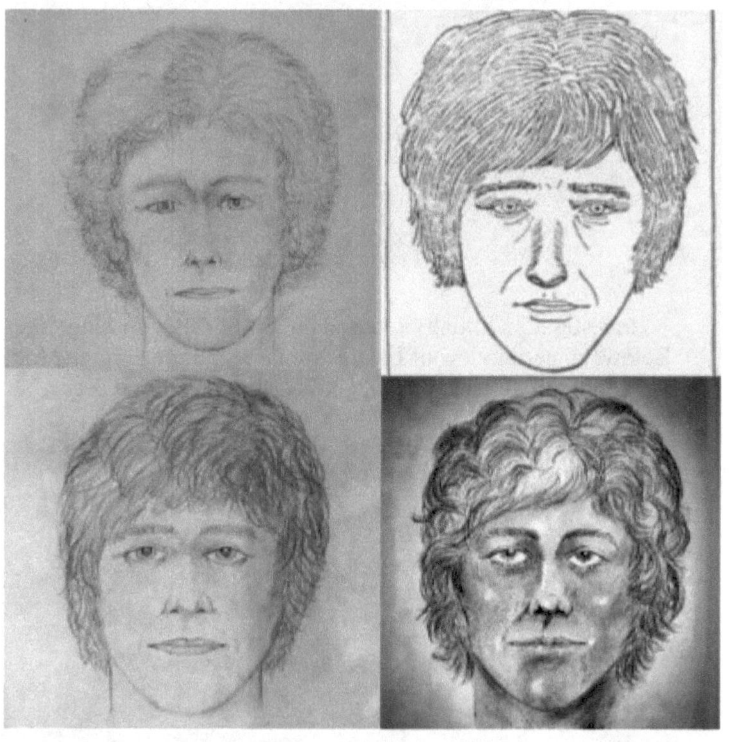

The many faces of "Ted"

Items found in Ted Bundy's car during his 1975 Utah arrest.
Below, his booking mug shot.

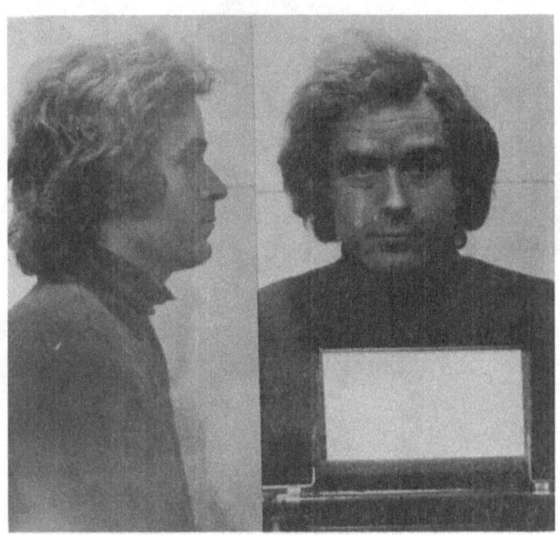

Carol DaRonch as she appeared during testimony in Bundy's 1976 trial for aggravated kidnapping.

The Fashion Place Mall in Murray, Utah, where Bundy approached Carol DaRonch. Below, DaRonch identified Bundy (second from right) during a routine police lineup.

Bundy abducted Caryn Campbell (above) from this hallway on the
2nd floor of the Wildwood Inn (below)

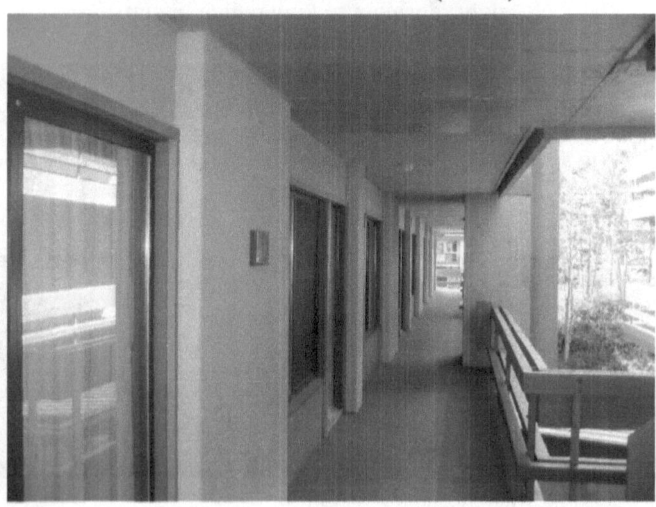

Bundy jumped out the window of the law library of the Pitkin County Courthouse in Aspen. Below, the wanted poster released by authorities after his escape.

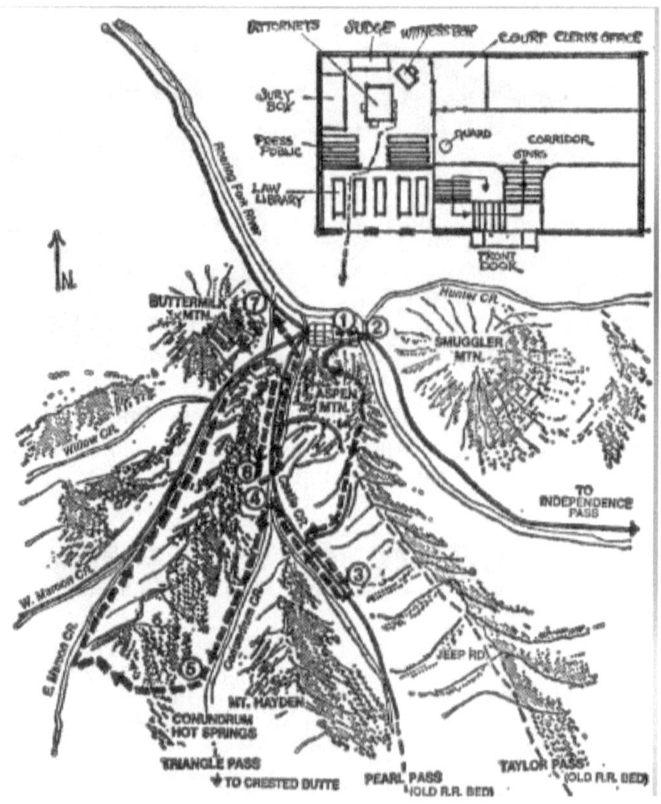

A map of the Aspen area law enforcement used to track Bundy after his escape.

Investigators stand outside a cabin believed to have been used by Bundy during his escape. Below, Bundy is all smiles after his capture.

Bundy's cell at the Glenwood Springs jail. He would again escape, this time through the light fixture in the ceiling.

October 3, 1975
Ex-Evans Campaign Aide Held in Utah Kidnaping

SALT LAKE CITY - Sheriff's deputies charged a 28-year-old former Tacoma resident here yesterday with kidnaping and attempted murder in connection with the abduction of a teen-age girl from a Murray shopping mall last year.

The suspect was identified as Theodore R. Bundy, a University of Utah law student who worked in 1972 as a member of Gov. Dan Evans' reelection campaign staff.

Bundy was arrested following a lineup at the Salt Lake City Jail yesterday morning and was arraigned before a city judge. Bail was set at $100,000.

Deputy Salt Lake County Attorney William R. Hyde placed a news blackout on the case after confirming that the charges stemmed from an incident Nov. 8, 1974, when a man posing as a police officer lured a 17-year-old girl into his car at gunpoint.

The man handcuffed the girl, but she managed to escape.

A key which fit the handcuffs was later found in the Bountiful High School parking lot where another girl, Debra Kent, 17, disappeared later that same day. Miss Kent has never been found.

Authorities said the girl who escaped with the handcuffs, as well as several witnesses to the incident, picked Bundy out in a police lineup.

Police also said they believed the mall incident was connected with the murders last year of Melissa Smith, 17, a daughter of the Midvale, Utah, police chief, and Laura Aime, 17, of Salem, Utah.

Miss Smith disappeared last Oct. 18 after leaving a restaurant. Her body, raped, beaten and strangled, was found Oct. 27 by deer hunters in Parley's Canyon not far from Salt Lake City.

Miss Aime's body was found Nov 27 in American Fork Canyon. She had also been strangled, beaten and raped. Miss Aime vanished from her home on a Friday night, the same night of the week Miss Smith had disappeared. Both bodies had nylon stockings around the necks.

Bundy worked as an advance man during Evans 1972 campaign and was employed for two months as an assistant to the Washington State Republican Central Committee, a job he left to attend the University of Utah.

One of Bundy's campaign assignments was to follow former Gov. Albert Rosellini to public meetings and news conferences and report back what was said. Bundy told newsmen at the time that he began as an unsalaried volunteer and that he posed as a college student working for a master's degree in political science.

Bundy went to work for the Republican state chairman as a volunteer in May 1973, was salaried part of the time and quit in August or September of that year in order to go to law school at the University of Puget Sound in Tacoma.

State GOP Chairman Ross Davis was stunned at the news of Bundy's arrest.

"He's such a neat guy. There has to be a mistake or something has happened. It's not the same guy I know."

Davis described Bundy as "an extremely friendly, likeable, able guy - I never heard anybody say anything bad about him. This just doesn't make any sense."

Bundy worked mostly inside the GOP headquarters, which was then in Olympia, primarily on mailings and reports.

October 3, 1975
Is Utah 'Ted' the Seattle 'Ted'?

Abduction and attempted murder charges against a former Seattle man in Utah yesterday brought to mind once more a series of abductions and slayings of young women in this area.

But Seattle police say they have been in touch with Utah authorities and do not consider the suspect involved there as a suspect in the so-called "Ted" slayings.

However, Capt. J. N. Mackie, who heads the investigation here, would not say the suspect had been "totally eliminated."

A witness who had seen the mysterious "Ted" involved with a young woman declared last night that a picture of the man charged in Utah was not the "Ted" she had seen.

Between January and June last year, at least seven young women disappeared from this general area. Skeletal remains of six of them have since been uncovered in secluded spots.

October 3, 1975
'Ted' Probers Get In Touch With Salt Lake City

Capt. J. N. (Nick) Mackie, commander of the King County Police Criminal Investigation Division, said last night he had been in contact with Salt Lake City authorities "for a considerable length of time" yesterday concerning Theodore Bundy, but Bundy was not considered a suspect in the so-called "Ted" slayings.

"At this time we have nothing to show that he is our 'Ted' suspect," Mackie told reporters as he left his office shortly after 5 p.m.

The suspect known as "Ted" had his arm in a sling and was interested in sailing. Asked whether these factors also applied to Bundy during the time of the "Ted" case last year, Mackle said, "Yes... but we get that on an awful lot of people."

Asked if Bundy has been "eliminated" as a suspect in the 'Ted' killings, Mackle replied: "No - he hasn't been totally eliminated."

Mackie said Bundy was merely "one of" the more than 2,800 persons who have been investigated at one time or another as "Ted" suspects.

He said he has no plans "at this time" to send detectives to Salt Lake City.

When a reporter asked Mackie if he considered it significant that Bundy had a truck with Washington plates, he replied. "I can't discuss anything about the Bundy case because he is under arrest in another jurisdiction."

Reporters who tried to contact Mackie yesterday afternoon were told he was "in a meeting" and could not be disturbed.

When Mackie emerged from his office last night and talked with reporters, he said the meeting had been with his two-person detective team assigned to the "Ted" investigation. Mackie said yesterday's meeting had been planned "for a couple of weeks."

He said the fact that the meeting came the day Bundy was arrested in Salt Lake City was only coincidence.

A spokesman for Police Chief Robert Hanson said last night:

"We will pursue all leads that develop, if any. The investigation into the deaths of the missing women in the so-called 'Ted' murders is continuing.

"We have no special comment on what we are doing at this time."

October 3, 1975
Witness Says Photo Unlike 'Ted'

A 23-year-old woman who saw the "Ted" suspect at Lake Sammamish State Park on July 14, 1974, said that a two-year-old photograph of Theodore Robert Bundy shows a man who is "too old" to be the "Ted" suspect she saw.

The woman was ono of several who were apparently approached by "Ted" at the park that day, the same day that Janice Ott and Denise Naslund disappeared and were later killed.

Asked whether the man in the photograph was too old, but could still resemble "Ted," the woman said, emphatically, "It's off, way off."

The woman stood on the porch of her Eastside home with her husband who said he did not want his wife to say any more. She said nothing more.

The woman is one of about half a dozen key witnesses in the case of seven women missing in this area last year. Six of the women have been confirmed dead after remains were found near Issaquah and at Taylor Mountain.

The witness was approached at Lake Sammamish State Park by a man in his early 20s who asked her to help him with his boat. He led her to his car, reportedly a brown Volkswagen. and opened the door to let her in but she refused to go with him. Her description matched other witnesses' reports on the man who was heard calling himself "Ted."

The remains of Ms. Ott and Ms. Naslund were recovered Sept. 7, 1974, 4.5 miles away from Lake Sammamish State Park near Interstate 90.

Other witnesses saw the "Ted" suspect at Lake Sammamish that day and at Ellensburg, April 17, 1974, the day that Susan Elaine Rancourt, 18, disappeared from the Central Washington State College campus. Ms. Rancourt's remains were found at Taylor Mountain near Issaquah March 3.

The fact that witnesses at Lake Sammamish and Ellensburg saw similar "Ted" suspects has been considered by police to be a key lead in the case.

October 3, 1975
The 'Ted' File Is Still Open

Charges against a Seattle area man in Salt Lake City in connection with the abduction and attempted murder of a girl there brought to mind a spree of abductions and killings of young women in the Seattle area.

Police here have been seeking a man named "Ted" in connection with the women's disappearance and the subsequent discovery of the skeletal remains of the six of them.

The Puget Sound-area mystery began Jan 31, 1974, when Lynda Ann Healy, 21, a University of Washington student vanished from her bedroom in the University District.

On March 12, Donna Gail Manson, 18, Auburn, failed to return to her room after a campus function at Evergreen State College in Olympia.

A month later, April 17, Susan Elaine Rancourt, 18, Anchorage, Alaska, disappeared from Central Washington State College in Ellensburg.

On May 6, Roberta Kathleen Parks, a 20-year-old Oregon State University co-ed from Lafayette, Calif. vanished but no connection was made at the time with the disappearances here - that grisly connection would be made almost 11 months later.

Brenda Ball, 22, was reported missing from the Burien area on June 1, last seen in a South End tavern.

It was on July 14 that the mysterious "Ted" - a smooth-talking young man with his arm in a cast or sling - asked two young women at Lake Sammamish Park, Janice Anne Ott, 23, and

Denise Marie Naslund, 18, to help him load a boat onto his VW Beetle. Neither was seen again, alive.

A massive search for "Ted' was launched by Seattle and King County Police, later to form a special "Ted" task force. The brown-haired young man, about 5 feet 8 inches tall and of medium build, became the prime suspect in the disappearance of seven of the eight missing women.

The first break in the case came Sept. 7, 1974, when two grouse hunters prowling the woods near Issaquah found what they thought were human bones.

Police combed the wooded area just off I-90, not far from Lake Sammamish, and eventually found skeletal remains of three persons.

Two were identified from dental records as Ms. Naslund and Ms. Ott. Police could not tell from the remaining bones even what sex the person was, let alone make an identification.

The search for "Ted" intensified but two months later, on Thanksgiving Eve, Vonnie Stuth, 19. disappeared from her South End home sometime between 11 p.m. when a relative spoke with her on the phone and 1:15 am when her husband returned home from work.

Had "Ted" struck again? For a while it appeared so but police later Found her body in the backyard of the Enumclaw home of Gary Addison Taylor, a one-time mental patient then being held in Texas where he is charged with rape and attempted rape.

Two Green River College forestry students were shocked last March 1 to find a skull while working on a project on Taylor Mountain near North Bend, about 10 miles from the place where Ms. Naslund's and Ms. Ott's remains were found.

A painstaking search of the area turned up skeletal remains later identified as those of Ms. Healy, Ms. Rancourt, Ms. Parks and Ms. Ball.

Since then, the 'Ted' task force has talked with more than 14,000 persons, investigated almost 3,000 "Teds" and checked out more than 1,000 suspect vehicles. But "Ted" remains as mysterious today as ever - unknown and unseen since a day in July of 1974 at Lake Sammamish State Park.

October 4, 1975
Bundy, "Ted' Link Still Pursued

SALT LAKE CITY - Police said here yesterday they have no evidence that either links Theodore R. Bundy with disappearances and murders of Seattle-area women last year or that indicates he is not the mysterious "Ted" suspected in those cases.

"We don't have a stitch of evidence either way," Salt Lake County Sheriff's Capt. Pete Hayward, chief of detectives, said of Bundy, 28, arrested here Thursday on kidnaping and attempted murder charges involving an attack on a young woman.

Hayward, interviewed yesterday, told The Post-Intelligencer that:

- Bundy was arrested Aug. 16 for possession of burglary tools and evading an officer - charges which led police to regard him as a suspect in the abduction case.
- An elaborate set of burglary tools, a ski mask and a pair of panty hose with eye and nose holes cut out were found in his brown Volkswagen at the time of the August arrest.
- Salt Lake City detectives "focused in' on Bundy about six weeks ago alter King County authorities notified them that Bundy had returned here from Washington state.

Bundy, who has remained silent but has obtained a lawyer following his arrest on the kidnaping and attempted murder charges, made a brief courtroom appearance yesterday.

A motion to reduce bail was scheduled to be heard, but it was inexplicably withdrawn and Bundy, wearing short hair in contrast to the shoulder-length style he previously wore, was returned to jail.

He is scheduled to enter a plea at a hearing at 2 p.m. Oct. 24.

When Bundy, campaign worker for Gov. Dan Evans in 1972 and former State Republican Central Committee employee, was arrested here Thursday, it raised speculation whether he could be the Seattle-area's "Ted."

Bundy drove a brown Volkswagen Beetle, as did "Ted."

Both "Ted" and Bundy have been described as handsome, easy talking and with longish hair. There are other similarities, but at least one King County witness who saw a picture of Bundy said he is not "Ted."

King County Detective Capt. Nick Mackie said yesterday that Bundy, being held on $100,000 bail here, is not a prime suspect in the Seattle-area cases. But he said Bundy hasn't been eliminated as a suspect.

Salt Lake County Capt. Hayward also said there is no evidence to link Bundy with the Washington disappearances and murders "But we certainly intend to find out," he said.

Hayward confirmed yesterday that detectives "focused in" on Bundy here about six weeks ago, which would be about the time the former Tacoma resident started his second year in law school at the University of Utah. Mackie's men alerted Salt Lake County police that Bundy had come here from Washington, Hayward said. He also confirmed that his men had been in Seattle to confer with King County detectives prior to Bundy's arrest here.

The captain said King County detectives had not come to Salt Lake City on the Bundy case. King County Public Safety Director Lawrence Waldt said yesterday he may send a detective here.

Hayward also revealed that Bundy first was arrested here about 2 a.m. last Aug. 16 while sitting in his brown VW Beetle in a residential neighborhood west of Salt Lake City.

State Patrol Sgt. Bob Hayward checked the auto and reported Bundy tried to flee in the car. The trooper stopped him and reported finding an elaborate set of burglary tools in Bundy's car.

Bundy was charged with two misdemeanors - evading an officer and possession of burglary tools. Both charges remain pending in addition to the two felony charges of kidnaping and attempted murder.

"Something connected with the misdemeanor charges led us to regard Bundy as a suspect in the abduction case," said Capt. Hayward. He would not say what the "something" was.

Capt. Hayward said Bundy spent one night in jail on the misdemeanor charges before posting bail.

The two felony charges came from a Nov. 8, 1974 incident at a shopping mall in suburban Murray.

Carol DaRonch, 18, at a police lineup Thursday, identified Bundy as the man who with a gun and a crowbar posed as a policeman, forced her into a brown VW Beetle, handcuffed her and drove off.

Ms. DaRonch managed to escape out a door with the handcuffs still on one wrist.

Later that same evening, Debra Kent, 17, of nearby Bountiful disappeared from a high school parking lot. She never has been found. Still later, a key fitting the handcuffs was found at the same parking lot.

Two murder cases are being investigated here but Capt. Hayward refused to call Bundy a suspect in either of them or even in the Kent girl's disappearance, despite the handcuffs and key tie-in.

But, before Bundy was arrested police said they regarded all the cases as being possibly connected.

The other two cases are those of Mellissa Smith, 17, daughter of Midvale police Chief Louis Smith, and Laura Anna Amie, also 17, of nearby Salem. Both girls disappeared last fall and their bodies were found later.

Capt. Hayward said Bundy had moved from one apartment to another and sold the brown (beige) VW within the past several weeks.

Detectives searched his new apartment after arresting him. They said it was "an ordinary male student's apartment." One thing found, the officers said, was a 2-foot square butcher block. Capt. Hayward said that shiny meat hooks attached to a ceiling held up a bicycle wheel in the kitchen from which pots and pans were suspended.

Police plan to impound the VW, an officer said.

They also found a 1953 pickup truck with Washington license plates that belongs to Bundy, officers said. In the back of the pickup were copies of the Wall Street Journal and a long-handled shovel.

Capt. Hayward said to his knowledge Bundy was not known to wear his arm in a sling or to have done any sailing down here. The Seattle-area "Ted" used a sling and boat with which he said he needed help as ruses to lure women into coming with him.

Regarding Bundy's Aug. 16 arrest, Sgt. Hayward said the suspect was "very cooperative" after he caught him.

The trooper said items found in the VW included a ski mask and a pair of panty hose with eye and nose holes cut out. Sgt. Hayward said Bundy informed him the apparent burglar tools were "just junk I'd collected." "He also said he had "just been out driving around at that hour," the trooper reported.

October 4, 1975
Police Had Bundy's Name in '74

King County police were given the name of Theodore R. Bundy as a possible suspect "not long" after two young women disappeared from Lake Sammamish State Park on July 14, 1974.

A young man known only as "Ted" was seen with one of them just before her disappearance.

Capt. J. N. (Nick) Mackie, commander of the King County Criminal Investigation Division, said yesterday, however, "no concrete evidence of any type" has been found to implicate Bundy with the murders of women in the Seattle arca - the so-called "Ted" slayings.

Bundy, a former Seattle, Tacoma and Olympia resident, was arrested in Salt Lake City Thursday and charged with the kidnaping and attempted murder of a teen-aged girl in Utah.

Bundy, former state employee, Republican Party official and University of Washington honors student, also is being questioned in connection with the murder of two more young girls in Utah. Mackie acknowledged yesterday similarities between the Bundy case and the "Ted" who may have figured in the 1974 disappearance of eight young women in the Northwest. Skeletal remains of six of them have been found in King County.

Mackie emphasized repeatedly in a news conference, however. Bundy is just one of more than 2.800 suspects turned up locally. Nothing has been found. Mackie said to give Bundy an alibi for the time of the Washington murders. "And we've got nothing to say he is involved," he stressed.

Bundy, 28, figured only casually in local investigations until Salt Lake City police started making inquiries about him more than a month ago, Mackie said.

"We have quite a few suspects who look very good," he said at one point. Later he said the list had about 30 names on it.

Mackie added that the two-man investigative team and sifted out another 100 or so names of suspects on which more information should be garnered. Bundy's name wasn't on the list.

Mackie said police were given Bundy's name "not long" after the women disappeared from Lake Sammamish State Park. An informant Mackie would not name advised county police that Bundy resembled composite drawings of the Lake Sammamish Ted suspect.

Initial investigation showed no reason to interview Bundy, Mackie continued, and county police still have not done so.

"I understand he's not talking to anyone now." Mackie said. "We're in close touch with Salt Lake police on this."

In summer 1974, police showed Bundy's picture to seven people who saw the Lake Sammamish Ted and none identified him. Recently, the same witnesses were shown other pictures of Bundy, and none picked him out. Mackie said. At one point in the investigation Bundy's name was one of 160,000 run through a computer to see if any had had prior associations with the missing and dead women. The computer said 38 had, but Bundy's wasn't one of them.

October 4, 1975
Bundy Told Of Work In Campaigns

Utah kidnapping and attempted-murder suspect Theodore R Bundy told Washington State Senate investigators in 1973 that he had worked on about half a dozen political campaigns including fulltime work for Art Fletcher's unsuccessful lieutenant-governor race in 1968 and Nelson Rockefeller's Republican presidential nomination drive the same year.

Senate investigators interviewed Bundy on Oct. 18, 1973, at the King County law library regarding his activities with Gov. Dan Evan's 1972 gubernatorial campaign.

The questioning was part of an investigation by state Sen. Gordon Sandison's Select Committee on Probable Cause into allegations that Evans campaign workers improperly observed gubernatorial candidate Albert Rosellini.

A summary of the interview was given to Sen. Pete Francis, Senate Judiciary Committee, and it remained on file.

Bundy said he went to public meetings where Rosellini spoke and tape-recorded his statements. He said he reported to Mary Ellen McCaffree with his work. Mrs. McCaffree is now head of the state Department of Revenue and then had charge of issues, research and strategy for Evans' campaign Headquarters.

Bundy said he met personally with Gov. Evans at a gathering at the Olympic Hotel, "to brief Evans on what Rosellini had said at a speech to the same gathering just prior to Evans' speech," the interviewers reported.

Bundy told interviewers Tony Cook, staff counsel with the Senate Research Center, and Capt. Jack Little, retired Bremerton police officer who worked for Sandison's committee, that he received $400 in compensation for his work with Evans' campaign.

Bundy said it was his idea to "keep track of Rosellini's public statements" and he started doing this at a Rosellini gathering at Edmonds Community College in Lynnwood.

He told the investigators he used a tape recorder because he had a bad memory. He said he never made any pretense of being a member of Rosellini's campaign.

"He never tried to hide the fact that he was an Evans person - he had Evans stickers on his car and both UPI and AP people knew of his Evans connection," the interview summary said.

Bundy said he was not promised future political jobs. "Bundy went on to say, that some were suspicious of his obtaining a job with the state (Republican) central committee this spring of 1973). However, Evans does not run the central committee, according to Bundy, and he obtained the job through other contacts," the interviewers reported.

Mrs. McCaffree said a number of young people attended Rosellini appearances for the Evans campaign, "mostly college students who had volunteered to go to public meetings to take down any statements and any questions."

Bundy was a law student at University of Puget Sound then, the interview record shows.

Mrs. McCaffree said Bundy's work was clandestine because "these were public meetings that they attended."

The committee was then investigating a larger scandal involving telephone records in which Bundy denied having any part.

October 5, 1975
Bundy's Seattle Friends Rally to Raise His Bail

SALT LAKE CITY - Theodore Robert Bundy held here since Thursday on Kidnaping and attempted-murder charges may be freed on bail soon possibly with the help of funds raised by Seattle friends.

Many friends in the Seattle area have asked if they can help, according to Marlin Vortman and attorney and friend of Bundy who arrived here yesterday.

Asked about bail raising Bundy's mother who lives in Tacoma, said she knew of no such plans but that Vortman would know.

A move on Friday to have Bundy s $100,000 bail lowered was suddenly withdrawn his attorney here said it was not certain how much bail money could be raised and until that was known no specific move would be made for a reduction.

Bundy is a former staff worker in Washington Gov. Dan Evans' 1972 re-election campaign but also has been identified with several other political efforts. He formerly served as special assistant to Republican State Chairman Ross Davis.

Bundy was charged Thursday with felony counts of kidnaping and attempted murder after a woman who escaped from her abductor picked him out of a police lineup Bundy previously been charged here with misdemeanor counts of possessing burglary tools and attempting to evade a police officer.

News of his arrest drew admissions from police of facials in King County Washington that Bundy's had been a suspect in the disappearance and slaying of a number of young women in the Seattle area but that he was not a prime suspect Since then authorities here and in Seattle have repeated that they have no evidence either linking Bundy to the so called "Ted".

Officers from Seattle are expected to confer with police here following the announcement Friday that detective "probably" would be sent.

Bundy's attorney John D O'Connell, formerly of Seattle. said he plans to move for a bail reduction later this week. Bundy actually appeared in city court there briefly for that purpose but was returned to his county jail cell with no court action taken.

Vortman, who said he has advised Bundy on matters previously, said he does not know if he will be defense counsel in the present case. He did not identify Bundy's friends who contacted him with offers of help but said "there are many of them".

Persons identified with Bundy either through politics or employment have been virtually uniform in their astonishment at his arrest. many of them expressing the view the view that there must be a mistake involved.

The Post-Intelligencer learned yesterday that Utah State Patrol and Salt Lake County officers reported finding a pair of Spanish-made handcuffs in the trunk of Bundy's beige-colored Volkswagen "bug" last August 16 when Bundy was arrested Just west of Salt Lake City.

That arrest came when an officer spotted Bundy, alone in the car, in a residential neighborhood late at night. As the officer approached, Bundy tried to flee but was caught. A charge of possession of burglary tools followed a search of the car. Bundy spent one night in jail before being released on bail.

Investigators here say that arrest incident led to Bundy's subsequent arrest and charges being placed against him in connection with a Nov 8, 1974 attempt by a man to abduct a young woman from a shopping mall. The man posed as a police officer and once he had the woman in his car - a brown Volkswagen - he handcuffed her. But she escaped, taking the handcuffs with her. Later that same day a young girl disappeared from a school parking lot with a search of the lot turned up a key that fit those same handcuffs. Police here said Bundy is due to appear at 2 pm Oct 24 to answer the kidnap and attempted. murder charges with the shopping mall incident. A former girlfriend, Tisha Weston, interviewed here, told The P.I. "I can't believe the charges against Ted. They must have the wrong man."

Ms. Weston recalls him as personable, kind, intelligent and a sophisticated talker. She said he liked to play tennis, ride bikes and told her he had friends in Washington with whom he used to go sailing in their boat.

But she also described Bundy as somewhat "aloof" - a man who never talked of his past, only the present and mostly the future."

The only time she recalled him being "upset" was when he told her last summer about a romance with a Stanford University girl, a romance that had broken up in 1973 or 1974, Ms. Weston said.

She described Bundy as being quite handsome - a man she believed could have all the female companionship he desired he had many girlfriends she said but she knew of no close ones with the exception of the Stanford woman.

October 5, 1975
Quest Goes On In Disappearance Of Area Women

Seattle and King County police continue their search for the person or persons responsible for the disappearance of a number of young women in this area. They have investigated to greater or lesser degrees, approximately 2,800 persons, acting on tips, phone calls and exhaustive detective work.

This past week officers were asked if they saw any connection between any of the disappearances and deaths and the arrest of a former area man in Utah. The official answer is that there is no evidence that there is a connection or that there is not.

Here is a recounting of the disappearances:

On July 14, 1974, a suave young man with his arm in a cast or sling approached at least five women at Lake Sammamish State Park and asked for assistance in loading a small boat onto his VW Beetle.

Two of those women, Janice Ann Ott, 23 and Denise Marie Naslund, 18, disappeared that day. Earlier, police had been puzzled by the disappearance of five other women from the Puget Sound area between Jan. 31 and June 11 but until the "Ted" incident no real connection between them had been made.

Lynda Ann Healy, 21, disappeared Jan. 31. 1974, from her University District rooming house; Donna Gail Manson, 19, vanished March 12 from Evergreen State College in Olympia; Susan Elaine Rancourt, 18, talked to a man like "Ted" April 17 on the Central Washington State College campus in Ellensburg and has not been seen since; Brenda Carol Ball, 22, Burien, was last seen June 1 in a South End tavern, and Georgann Hawkins, 18, vanished from the alley behind her UW sorority house, June 11.

On May 6, Roberta Kathleen Parks, 20, an Oregon State University co-ed, also disappeared but at first there seemed to be no relationship between that and cases here.

The skeletal remains of Ms. Naslund, Ms. Ott and a third person were discovered Sept. 7. 1974, in a wooded area off I-90 near Issaquah, not far from Lake Sammamish. The two women were identified by dental records, but police could not determine the sex of the bones of a third body.

Last March 1 another grisly find about 10 miles away near Taylor Mountain accounted for Ms. Healy, Ms. Rancourt, Ms. Parks and Ms. Ball.

October 7, 1975
Bundy in Jail 'Till Press Goes'

SALT LAKE CITY - The attorney for former Tacoman Theodore Bundy, charged with kidnaping and attempted murder here, said yesterday that his client will remain in jail until the press goes away.

"If the publicity is too bad, we don't want him out," John O'Connell, Bundy's attorney, told the P-I.

O'Connell also said he will meet with the county prosecuting attorney sometime today to discuss "how we will handle this case so it is orderly."

Referring to Bundy remaining in jail until publicity dies down, the attorney said:

"The jail is as good a place to hide any place," O'Connell said. "I don't know who is out there who wants to kill him," O'Connell said, but under questioning he added that no threats had been received on Bundy's life that he was aware of. "What we're hoping is that you'll all go away," O'Connell said of the press.

"At this point he is content to stay in jail," O'Connell said when asked what Bundy thought of being in jail on $100,000 bail.

"We're just trying to determine what the situation is and where to go from here," O'Connell said. "It is hard to separate out and see what the real case is amidst all the talk." Asked if the arrest of Bundy might be a case of mistaken identity, O'Connell said he did not want to answer questions about the case. Bundy was picked out of a police lineup by Carol DaRonch, 17, as the man who abducted her at gunpoint and threatened to kill her.

O'Connell had said earlier that he might try to have the ball reduced this week but yesterday he said no decision has been made on whether to go ahead with that plan. The relatively high bail is caused "by all the speculation," O'Connell said.

Under Utah law, the preliminary hearing on the charges against Bundy in city court October 24 may be closed to the public, as may the trial in district court if one is held. O'Connell said that the hearing will probably be open to the public. "If it isn't, the press gets upset," he said.

Bundy was baptized a member of the Mormon church Aug. 30, some two weeks after his first encounter with police when they stopped him and found what they say were burglary tools in his brown Volkswagen. He had applied to work as a security guard at the University of Utah this September.

The job involves opening and locking doors and turning lights on and off, according to campus security chief Wayne Shepherd.

He interviewed Bundy for the job knowing that Salt Lake authorities had him under investigation for possession of burglary tools. That charge is still pending.

"He was very intelligent. Brilliant. Very smooth. He could win a person over very easily," Shepard said of the interview.

Campus security made its own check on him, Shepard said, but ran into dead ends trying to find people who knew him well. "I don't know if he just didn't get involved here. As likeable as the guy seemed to be, you'd think there would be somebody," Shepard said. He did not get the job as a guard but was given one as a university custodian starting about the first of September this year, Shepard said.

He did not get the job as a guard but was given one as a university custodian starting about the first of September this year, Shepard said.

Gerald Thompson, Salt Lake County sheriff's detectives said Seattle police detective Ted Fonis and King County Sheriff's detective Robert Keppel were in Salt Lake City over the weekend on a fact-finding mission in the case but did not speak to Bundy.

Thompson said Seattle and Salt Lake police are not conducting any joint investigation of crimes in their areas but officers in those states as well as Colorado and California where women have also been murdered have been routinely exchanging field reports during the past year.

"We'll cooperate with Seattle, but this has nothing to do with Seattle's investigation whatsoever," Thompson said.

October 9, 1975
The Bundy Arrest: A Fluke

SALT LAKE CITY - The Utah State Highway patrolman who arrested Theodore R. Bundy for possession of burglary tools and trying to evade an officer on Aug. 16 said yesterday he had not heard of Bundy before that night. Sgt. Bob Hayward, who apprehended Bundy, a former Tacoma resident, at 3 a.m. in a Salt Lake City suburb 15 miles from home dressed in a black turtleneck shirt, Levis and sneakers, said the arrest came about by accident.

Hayward is the brother of the man now in charge of the Salt Lake County sheriff's investigation of the Bundy case, Capt. N. D. (Pete) Hayward.

The trooper said he could not recall his brother Pete ever mentioning Bundy's name before the arrest.

As the trooper described the arrest, he was sitting in his unmarked car on duty in front of his own house just before his shift was to end when a Volkswagen which he did not recognize drove by him.

Hayward, who said he always patrols his own neighborhood the last few minutes of his shift, said he ignored the Volkswagen, but about ten minutes later he responded to a call which took him around the corner where the Volkswagen parked.

"He wasn't 200 yards from my house," Hayward said, and as he drove up beside the car, he directed his searchlight on it. "He took off like a shot with no lights on and the chase was on," Hayward said. "If he had sat in that Volkswagen, I probably would have driven right past him," he said.

Bundy drove through two stop signs, one after Hayward had turned on his red light. Finally, Bundy pulled into a service station and stopped, Hayward said.

When the trooper asked him why he had tried to flee, Bundy replied that he was frightened and did not know who the trooper was, Hayward related.

When Hayward asked Bundy what he was doing in the neighborhood at that hour, Bundy answered that he had been to a drive-in theatre and had become lost. Asked what movie he had seen, Bundy said it was "The Towering Inferno." A check of area theatres found none showing that film, Hayward said. The passenger seat of Bundy's Volkswagen had been removed and placed in the back seat, Hayward said, and some burglary tools, including an icepick were found on the passenger side.

Also found in the car were a nylon stocking, a ski mask and a pair of handcuffs.

County police arrived and questioned Bundy again about what he was doing in the neighborhood at that time of night "dressed like that," Hayward said. "Nothing added up." Hayward said of Bundy's explanations. Hayward said that at the time he did not attach any significance to the Volkswagen, even though one had been used during the kidnap and attempted murder Bundy later was charged with.

Nor did Hayward attach any significance to the nylon stocking or ski mask except as possible disguises in armed robberies which had occurred in the neighborhood.

Nylon stockings were found around the throats of two girls raped and murdered last fall in Salt Lake City.

Hayward said that after the arrest he called his brother and told him about it.

From that incident, two misdemeanor charges were logged against Bundy, one involving possession of burglary tools, which is entered on the docket for Nov 11 in Murray City Court, and the other involving evading an officer. The latter charge is pending in Granger City Court.

Capt. Pete Hayward said yesterday he was notified by Seattle Police sometime during the spring quarter of this school year that Bundy was among suspects in cases involving women missing or killed in the Seattle area and that he had moved to Salt Lake City.

Asked if Bundy might be charged with other crimes in Salt Lake City, the captain replied, "At this point, I know of nothing."

Hayward said investigation into the deaths of two murdered Salt Lake City girls and one missing girl is continuing, however.

The two girls were found raped, beaten and strangled with a nylon stocking. Prior to Bundy's arrest police had said they believed the two deaths and the case of the missing girl were related.

The kidnapping and attempted murder charges against Bundy came from a Nov. 8, 1974 incident at a shopping mall in Murray.

Carol DaRonch, 18, identified Bundy at a police lineup last week as the man who forced her into a brown VW Beetle, handcuffed her and drove off.

Ms. DaRonch managed to escape out a door with the handcuffs still on one wrist.

Later that same evening, Debra Kent, 17, of nearby Bountiful, disappeared from a high school parking lot. She has never been found. Still later, a key fitting the handcuffs was found in the same parking lot.

Ms. DaRonch was one of three witnesses who picked Bundy out of a lineup last week. Another was a teacher who said she had been approached by a man who tried to get her to come in his car during a school play which Miss Kent was also attending just before she disappeared.

Bundy is being held in jail here on $100,000 bail.

October 10, 1975
Area Where Bundy Lived Scoured
Probe of Missing Women 'Picks Up'

The probe of missing and murdered women in this area has picked up" since the arrest in Salt Lake City on Oct. 2 of Theodore R. Bundy, a police official said yesterday.

Detectives yesterday used a metals detector to search the grounds of a house at 4143 12th Ave. NE, where Bundy rented a room from about 1970 through August of 1974. when he left to attend the University of Utah law school in Salt Lake City.

King County Sheriff's Detective Capt. Nick Mackle said through a spokesman that the investigation has "picked up." But he declined to say what detectives were hunting for with the metal detector, which was used around flower beds and lawn areas of the University District home owned by Mrs. Freida Roger.

The sheriff's spokesman said the deputy prosecuting attorney on the case of the missing, and murdered women here had ordered officers not to discuss any aspects of the probe with newsmen "because an investigation is underway." Deputy Prosecuting Attorney Phillip Kileen confirmed that he had issued such a directive. He said he would not comment any further, except to add that "I don't know anything about the Ted Bundy case."

Officers who were at Mrs. Roger's place yesterday morning also checked out storage places, including a garage in back of the house. There was no indication if they found anything.

Mrs. Roger, who has described Bundy as an exceptionally nice person, said she didn't know what the detectives were looking for. She said she had never noticed anything unusual in Bundy's second-floor room on his person or his auto.

Bundy, former campaign staff worker for Gov. Dan Evans and former aide to State Republican Central Committee Chairman Ross Davis, is in Salt Lake County jail charged with kidnaping and attempted murder in connection with a Utah case in which a man forced a young woman into his car last Nov 8. She managed to escape.

Bundy's arrest in Salt Lake City raised speculation here about possible links between Utah and Seattle cases. The sheriff's office here has said that while Bundy was not a prime suspect in the Seattle area cases, he had been one of 2,800 suspects in the so- called "Ted" murders of young women in the area.

Yesterday, the Mackie spokesman said the probe here "has picked up" since Bundy was arrested and charged with the Utah offences. The search of the grounds and garage where Bundy formerly roomed in the University District was evidence of this.

The sheriff's department has added one more detective to its "Ted" task force, making it a three-person unit.

The Seattle Police Department has put two officers back on the probe. One formerly was on the county-city task force and he and his partner were assigned to the stepped-up investigation that followed Bundy's arrest.

But the sheriff's and city police detectives are only "coordinating" their efforts now. Previously, the city detectives worked directly under Mackie and were housed in the county courthouse.

A Seattle police spokesman said the new arrangement doesn't reflect any difficulties between the two police departments only the fact that the earlier task force had been disbanded.

But an authoritative source told The Post-Intelligencer that there had been "difficulties" between the two departments regarding the "Ted" probe and that city police intended to pursue any possible Bundy connection, regardless of what county police do.

Mrs. Roger, who talked to detectives yesterday at her house, said she understood that Bundy had been engaged to a woman named Elizabeth, who had a small daughter. Mrs. Roger said she had seen Elizabeth, but that Bundy wasn't the one who said they were engaged.

Bundy wore a beard about the time Gov. Dan Evans had one in late 1973, Mrs. Roger said, adding that Bundy shaved the beard off, apparently late that year or early 1974.

Meanwhile, a woman who says she saw the mysterious "Ted" at Lake Sammamish State Park on July 14, 1974 said yesterday that Bundy, with a haircut, does not look at all like "Ted".

She saw pictures of Bundy, taken in Utah after his longish hair had been trimmed in jail there.

"He looks older and there's the start of a receding hairline," she said of the short-hair photos. "The man I saw was younger and with no receding hairline," she explained.

A man who called himself "Ted" approached her at Lake Sammamish and asked if she'd help him put a sailboard atop his tan Volkswagen Beetle. The woman has told authorities she refused to get into his auto when he said the boat was some distance away up the hill.

Jan Ott, 23 and Denise Naslund, 19, later disappeared from the park and their remains were found near Issaquah about three miles away.

Mrs. Roger said Bundy had a boat, but it was an inflatable raft he sometimes carried in the VW's trunk. She said she never saw him with a sailboat and doesn't think he ever had one.

Another acquaintance recalled going on a rafting trip with Bundy and others in June 1974.

October 11, 1975
Bundy Off Job When 2 Women Vanished

Theodore R. Bundy was absent from his state job in Olympia two days prior to and two days after the July 1974 weekend on which Jan Ott, 23, and Denise Naslund, 19, were abducted from Lake Sammamish State Park, records show.

The two women vanished from the park on Sunday July 14.

Meanwhile King County police have issued an all-points bulletin. asking Western states police departments for any information they have on Bundy or his automobile.

Information requested includes any interrogation reports. parking and traffic tickets and any other cases involving Bundy or the auto.

King County Detective Capt. Nick Mackie said Thursday that the investigation of missing and murdered women in this area has picked up" since Bundy was arrested in Salt Lake City Oct 2 and charged with kidnaping and attempted murder in an abduction attempt of a young woman in suburban Murray. The woman escaped after being forced into an auto Nov. 8, 1974.

The sparse remains of Ms. Ott and Ms. Naslund, who were taken from Lake Sammamish State Park on Sunday, July 14, 1974, were found about three miles from Issaquah the following Sept. 7. Remains of a third, unidentified person also were found.

A mysterious man who called himself "Ted" was seen leaving the Lake Sammamish beach area with Ms. Ott that day wearing his right arm in a sling or cast. "Ted" asked Ms. Ott and several other women to help him put his sailboat atop his auto, a light brown Volkswagen beetle.

Six other young women disappeared from this area in 1974 prior to the Lake Sammamish incidence. Remains of four of them, in addition to those of Ms. Ott and Ms. Naslund have been found in eastern King County.

Neil Miller, administrative officer of the state department of emergency services, where Bundy worked the summer of 1974, said yesterday Bundy was absent from work on Thursday and Friday, June 11 and 12th and Monday and Tuesday, July 15 and 16th.

Ms. Ott left the park around noon that July 14 Sunday, wheeling her yellow bike along as she talked with Ted. The bike has never been found.

Ms. Naslund vanished from the park four hours later. Witnesses put Ted back in the park during the afternoon again asking women to help with his sailboat.

Asked why Bundy was off his state job on the above dates, Miller said, he phoned in sick.

Miller said records didn't indicate the nature of the illness and that Bundy was back on the job Wednesday, July 17. He took sick leave July 11, but was off without pay the other three days because he didn't have enough accrued sick leave, Miller explained.

Miller remembered that one time during the summer, Bundy "had a real bad cold" but couldn't say if it was during mid-July.

Asked if she knew the nature of her son's illness in mid-July, his mother, Mrs. John Bundy of Tacoma, said, "I know exactly where he was at that time, but you're not the one I would tell it to."

She said she had no comment for the press on the absences.

Bundy worked in the department from May 23 through August 28, 1974, leaving to enroll in law school at the University of Utah. He was a second-year law student when arrested October 2 in Salt Lake City.

The young woman who escaped it would be a doctor in Murray November 8, 1974 has identified Bundy as her assailant.

Asked about other absences, Miller said Bundy also was out sick on June 17, June 24, and July 1, 1974.

The disappearance of started here when Linda Ann Healey, 21, vanished from a university district rooming house on January 31 or February 1, 19 74.

On March 12, Donna Gail Manson, 18, from Auburn, disappeared from the Evergreen State College campus in Olympia.

On April 17, Susan, Elaine Rancourt, 18, from Anchorage, Alaska, vanished from the central Washington state college in Ellensburg.

On May 6, Roberta, Kathleen Parks, 20, disappeared from Oregon State University, Corvallis. She was from Lafayette, California.

Brenda Ball, 22, turned up missing on June 1 from the Burien area where she lived and last had been seen in a tavern.

On June 31, Georgina Hawkins, Lakewood, vanished in a well-lit alley in the university district.

October 12, 1975
"Bundy We Know Couldn't Do That" -- Missionaries

SALT LAKE CITY - The Mormon missionaries who baptized Theodore R Bundy August 30 said Friday they had never seen anything in his behavior that would suggest he was about to be charged with kidnaping and attempted murder.

"I wouldn't hesitate to line him up with my sister," is the way Larry Anderson, one of the missionaries, said it.

The 27-year-old Anderson who converted Bundy said that he and his missionary companion John Homer introduced Bundy to several girls and had double-dated with him.

"The Ted Bundy we know couldn't do that reference to kidnap and murder attempt charges unless he was two people. He would have to be two people," Anderson said.

Bundy, 28. is being held here on $100,000 bail on charges he abducted 18-year-old Carol DaRonch from a Salt Lake City parking lot Nov 8. 1974 while posing as a policeman. and handcuffed and threatened to kill her She escaped and was one of three persons to identify Bundy in a police lineup.

Bundy was arrested Aug. 16 of this year on possession of burglary tools and evading an officer but he did not tell either of the missionaries of that arrest, they said in a P.I. interview.

Homer said that Bundy was very concerned about ethical behavior and "nothing but a gentleman all the time."

But Homer said that he had not been able to satisfy himself about what Bundy was doing the early morning hours of Aug 16 when he was arrested. "That seems weird," Homer said.

Bundy was dressed in a black turtleneck, Levis, and sneakers when he was first arrested which Anderson said was Bundy's usual dress.

Anderson and Homer said they have seen Bundy several times since he has been in jail, but they have never talked with him about the charges against him "We haven't wanted to talk to him about it," Anderson said.

"He's not in a jovial mood, but he definitely feels justice will be done." Anderson related. He said Bundy is alone in a cell.

The first time they visited him, he was really upset and would not talk, Anderson said.

"He just kept shaking his head and saying, 'I don't understand what's happening,'" Homer said.

"Right now, I think he feels protected in the jail from people who have already decided he is guilty," Anderson said.

The first thing he asked for was a Bible and the Book of Mormon. He said he was thankful for his God and his church. "I can't see a maniac being too thankful for anything," said Anderson, who has a degree in psychology.

On their most return visit Bundy told them, "'I'm winning the chess tournament.' Then he broke down," Anderson said.

Bundy, who is broke according to the missionaries, has been worried about how he will pay for his defense and Anderson said someone from Washington has guaranteed to Bundy's attorney that his fees will be paid.

Anderson said that he and Bundy and Homer had discussed the abductions and murders of two 17-year-old Salt Lake City girls whose nude, raped and strangled bodies were found last fall in nearby canyons. But Bundy expressed no more than an ordinary person's interest in those events.

"I'm not one who believes in having a guy put in jail when he does a thing like that. I'd want him shot. I believe in capital punishment and so does Ted," Anderson said.

Bundy returned here from Seattle this summer to start classes at U of Utah law school, they said. They first met him last November during a church-initiated "Project Search" for new members for a campus branch of the Mormon Church, Anderson said.

From November to February, Bundy had only an "academic" interest in Mormonism. "His conversion came much later," Anderson said.

About February, he began to attend church and was very active in related social church functions until the end of the school year when he returned to Washington State, they said.

The declined to relate the specific circumstances of his conversion but Anderson said, "It was just a testimony building in a guy. He just progressed normally for a guy who is really looking." Bundy knew a great deal about the Bible, Anderson added.

They described Bundy as an antique buff, a gourmet cook, and a lover of classical music. "His kitchen was really a showplace. It wouldn't seem strange for Ted to have an icepick when you see what he cooks with," Anderson said. An icepick was found in his car the night of his first arrest.

Anderson said that Bundy's blue parka and some of his cassette tapes have been sent to the FBI laboratories in Washington, D.C.

Bundy sold his tan Volkswagen recently and moved to a less expensive apartment so he would have enough money to go to school, they said.

They said that Bundy had told them he wanted to be a lawyer because "he got interested in politics in Washington State. He felt that he really had a knack for politics, and he felt that the way to be in was through law."

January 2, 1976
Bundy Allowed to See Photos

SALT LAKE CITY - Theodore R. Bundy, charged with kidnaping a suburban Murray woman more than a year ago, has won the right to inspect photos of him shown to the woman when she identified him as her abductor.

District Judge Peter F. Leary granted the request, made by Bundy's attorney, John D. O'Connell on Wednesday, but refused the defence permission to conduct discovery proceedings for other photos, or rumoured police reports, that defines attorneys claim were available from law enforcement agencies. O'Connell said law enforcement officials other than Murray police had questioned the alleged kidnap victim, Carol DaRonch, 18, who lives in Murray, south of Salt Lake City. O'Connell had sought to see these reports, as well as other Bundy identification photos.

Bundy, 29, formerly of Tacoma and a second-year law student at the University of Utah here when arrested Oct. 2 on the kidnaping charge, had about a three-weeks growth of beard when he and his attorney appeared in the judge's chambers yesterday, asking for information the county prosecuting attorney might have. Bundy, who was active in Republican politics in his home state, is scheduled to go on trial on the kidnaping charge on Feb. 9 here.

Deputy Pros. Atty. David Yocom said his files include only two instances in which photos of Bundy were shown, and that he has reports on these instances. He offered to hand the reports to O'Connell. Both instances "involve showing the photos to Miss DaRonch," Yocom said. Both showings occurred before an Oct. 2 police line-up, at which Miss DaRonch reportedly identified Bundy as her alleged abductor. O'Connell also asked for photos furnished to Utah authorities by King County police, but Yocom said he would have to check with the King County prosecuting attorney on the request.

O'Connell also pressed Yocom on what the defence attorney hinted might be "weaknesses" in Miss DaRonch's testimony at a preliminary hearing last November. A companion charge of attempted homicide, stemming from the same abduction incident, was dismissed after that hearing. O'Connell said yesterday that Miss DaRonch had indicated at the November hearing, which was closed to the public and press, that she experienced some difficulty in identifying Bundy from photos as her abductor. Yocom said a transcript of the preliminary hearing would be provided the judge. The judge said he would study the transcript, then decide whether to grant additional defense discovery requests.

Yocom said he does not want to file the preliminary hearing transcript with the county clerk because then it would become a public record, subject to anyone's perusal. O'Connell, who asked for the closed preliminary hearing, agreed to keeping the transcript secret. Bundy has been investigated in connection with a number of abductions and slayings of young women in King County, in Utah and in Colorado. However, authorities say they have no evidence linking him with those crimes.

January 17, 1976
Wednesday Hearing in Bundy Case

SALT LAKE CITY - A motion by Theodore Bundy's defense counsel to suppress a police lineup identification of him by his alleged kidnap victim will be argued in court here Wednesday. Bundy's trial on charges of kidnaping a 19-year-old suburban Murray woman in November 1974, is scheduled for Feb. 9 here. He has pleaded innocent to the charge.

Defense counsel Bruce C. Lubeck filed the motion to suppress the identification testimony of the alleged victim on grounds the police line- up was improper because everyone in the lineup except Bundy was a policeman. This would make it more likely the woman would identify the non-policeman: in the view of the defense. The motion says pre-trial confrontations between Bundy and his alleged victim, Carol DaRonch, "were conducted in such an impermissibly suggestive manner as to give rise to a very substantial likelihood of irreparable misidentification."

District Judge Stewart Hanson Jr. set a hearing on the motion for 1:30 p.m. Wednesday. Authorities have said Bundy has been investigated in connection with disappearances or deaths of other young women in Washington State, Utah and Colorado but that they have no evidence linking him to those cases.

January 22, 1976
Hearing on Bundy to Resume Today

SALT LAKE CITY - (AP) - A closed hearing on a motion by Theodore R. Bundy to suppress eyewitness identification of him by his alleged kidnap victim will resume today. The hearing was recessed yesterday after newsmen and the public were excluded from the district court proceedings by request of John O'Connell, defense attorney. Utah law provides for such closed court hearings.

Bundy, charged with aggravated kidnaping in the alleged abduction in suburban Murray of Carol DaRonch, then 18, more than a year ago, has pleaded innocent. His trial is scheduled to begin, here Feb. 9. The defense motion to suppress DaRonch's identification in a police lineup of Bundy Oct. 2 was made on grounds everyone in the lineup except Bundy was a policeman. The motion also contends confrontations between Bundy and DaRonch "were conducted in such an impermissibly suggestive manner as to give rise to a very substantial likelihood of irreparable misidentification."

Bundy appeared at the hearing, wearing a full beard he said he's been growing about a month. Bundy also faces trial in Murray on a date not yet set on a charge of attempting to evade a state patrolman last Aug. 16 near Salt Lake City.

February 24, 1976
Witness Picks Out Bundy

SALT LAKE CITY - A sobbing woman witness looked across the courtroom yesterday and identified Theodore R. Bundy as the man who kidnaped and threatened to kill her here Nov. 8, 1974.

Bundy remained relaxed and impassive as Carol DaRonch, 19, picked him out. However, Bundy stared at her intently most of the time she testified during the first day of his non-jury kidnaping trial.

Bundy, 29, formerly of Seattle and Tacoma and recently a University of Utah law student, was neatly dressed in white shirt, dark tie and light grey suit. He was clean-shaven in contrast to a full beard he wore for several months.

Ms. DaRonch said the man identified as Bundy approached her at a suburban Murray shopping mall.

She said he told her someone had looted her car and got her to go with him in his light beige 1968 Volkswagen bug to report the matter to police. She said she became suspicious of the man, who told her he was a policeman, but felt less concerned after he showed her a badge in his wallet.

A half-mile from the shopping center, the man stopped his car and without a word snapped handcuffs on one wrist, she said.

She resisted and he was unable to cuff the other wrist. She said she tried to get out of the car.

"I was screaming, asking him what he was doing," she sobbed. "Then he pulled a gun, a small black one and said he would blow my brains out.

"I got out the door and he slid across the seat after me. I was screaming as loud as I could and scratching him (with her fingernails)."

Outside the car she said the man raised a pry bar in his right hand and tried to strike her, but she grabbed his arm.

She managed to break free and ran out into the street. where she was picked up by a couple in a car. She said she was hysterical.

The woman identified Bundy last Oct. 2 in a police lineup here. Bundy was arrested that day and charged with the kidnaping.

Defense Attorney John D. O'Connell said in his opening statement that "we do not have a cold alibi," but that the defense would show Bundy was not at the Murray mall that Nov,8.

O'Connell also asked the 'judge to look carefully at Ms. DaRonch; the attorney characterized her as "immature, unsophisticated and vague." He said she was "submissive to authority a person who does what she's told." He added that when "push comes to shove, she will fight."

During cross-examination of Ms. DaRonch, O'Connell showed that she didn't remember some things well, and he had her admit she wasn't able to make a positive identification, of Bundy from photos shown her.

She also gave differing testimony on identification of Bundy's auto at a previous hearing, O'Connell showed, including where rust spots were and the exact color.

But in the main the slender brunette, with her long brown hair parted in the middle, stuck to her story and was emphatic that she recognized Bundy as her assailant upon first seeing him Oct. 2.

February 25, 1976
UW Prof to Testify In Bundy Trial

SALT LAKE CITY - A Seattle woman will be called by the defense as an expert on eyewitness identification in the Theodore R. Bundy kidnaping trial here today.

Dr. Elizabeth Loftus, a University of Washington psychology professor who has been on temporary duty at Harvard will be here today, defense attorney John O'Connell told Third District Judge Steward Hanson Jr.

As a defense witness, Dr. Loftus could be expected to cast doubt on Monday's eyewitness identification of Bundy by Carol DaRonch, 19, of suburban Murray, the alleged kidnap victim.

From the witness stand here Monday Ms. DaRonch said Bundy is the man who abducted her from a Murray mall Nov. 3, 1974, snapped handcuffs on one wrist, pointed a gun at her head, and threatened to kill her. then tried to strike with a crowbar before, she broke free.

Bundy, a 1972 graduate of the University of Washington, majored in psychology but it is not known if he was a student of Dr. Loftus.

A former campaign aide to Gov. Dan Evans and former state Republican Party aide and state employee, Bundy, 29, has waived trial by jury and Judge Hanson will decide the case. Bundy, most recently a law student at the University of Utah. was arrested on the kidnap charge here last Oct. 2.

Mr. and Mrs. Wilbur Walsh of Murray, the couple who picked up Ms. DaRonch after she escaped her abductor, testified yesterday it was an eerie experience. Mrs Walsh said:

"This young girl appeared out of the mist, into our headlights. She pulled a door of our car open (and jumped in).

"This child was in such a state that we let her in. I have never seen a human being so frightened, so terrified. I put my arm around her... not until I held her tight, and told her she was safe, did she cry: 'He was going to kill me if I didn't stop screaming. He was going to kill me.'"

Walsh's testimony paralleled that of his wife. Other witnesses yesterday included police officers who testified about various facets of the Bundy case.

Bundy was stopped Aug. 16, 1975 by Utah State Highway patrolman Robert Hayward, who testified yesterday he and other officers found a crowbar like that described by Ms. DaRonch, in Bundy's Volkswagen bug. They also found a pair of handcuffs, Sargent Hayward said.

O'Connell is seeking to show Ms. DaRonch's identification of Bundy stems from the power of suggestion, resulting from police showing her such things as pictures of him and of his car. She identified Bundy in an Oct. 2 police lineup.

O'Connell has succeeded in showing some conflicts in earlier statements made by Ms. DaRonch and some police witnesses with their trial testimony.

The defense also has resisted a state "implication" that dried blood found on Ms. DaRonch's jacket from her scratching her assailant could be Bundy's.

A laboratory report found the jacket blood to be type O but couldn't determine if it was positive or negative. A blood sample taken from Bundy tested out as type O positive and a sample from Ms. DaRonch was type A positive.

O'Connell declared about half the male population has type O blood. He also insisted the jacket blood could have been so dried it would test type O even though it actually had been another type.

February 26, 1976
Bundy To Testify in His Trial

SALT LAKE CITY - Theodore R. Bundy will testify at his kidnaping trial here, he said, as the state rested yesterday and the defense began calling witnesses. The trial, which began Monday, may end this week.

University of Washington psychology professor Elizabeth Loftus took the stand yesterday after the defense won a battle with the prosecution on whether she should be heard as an expert on eyewitness identification.

Dr. Loftus testified that eyewitness identification can be uncertain, especially under extreme stress or following passage of time. Innocent bystanders who become familiar to witnesses' sight are apt to be picked as suspects through what she called "unconscious transference."

Deputy county attorney David Yocom, on cross examination, asked what she was getting for testifying yesterday. She replied that her expert witness fee was $150 for the day plus all expenses and roundtrip airfare to Salt Lake City. Judge Stewart Hanson took under advisement a motion by defense attorney John O'Connell to reduce the charge against Bundy from aggravated kidnaping to kidnaping. Mr. and Mrs. John Bundy, Tacoma, the defendant's parents, were in the courtroom for the first time yesterday, sitting directly behind their son. The parents of the accuser, Mr. and Mrs. Frank A. DaRonch, and a son, Frank Jr., sat on the opposite side of the courtroom. Carol DaRonch, the alleged kidnap victim, was not present. DaRonch had testified previously that Bundy is the man who, posing as a policeman, lured her into his Volkswagen in Murray Nov. 8, 1974, snapped handcuffs one wrist, threatened to shoot her and then tried to strike her with a crowbar. At that point. said, she broke free and was rescued by a couple that happened to drive by.

Other witnesses yesterday included several friends and neighbors of Bundy. They testified they had never seen a crowbar or handcuffs in his auto.

February 27, 1976
Bundy Lied to Police, Lawyer; Cites Paranoia

SALT LAKE CITY - Testimony ended yesterday in the kidnaping trial of Theodore Bundy after the defendant admitted on the witness stand that he lied to police and his own attorney.

Bundy, on the stand two hours, said he was smoking marijuana the night of last Aug. 15-16 when first arrested by police here for possession of burglary tools.

His "paranoia" about getting caught smoking pot caused him to lie to police and his attorney by reporting he'd been to a movie at a nearby drive-in that night, he explained. He said he had been to no movie.

He said his "paranoia" stemmed from a fear that getting caught smoking pot could affect his law studies at the University of Utah.

When a state patrolman spotted Bundy's car parked in a residential neighborhood, after Bundy's car had twice passed the officer's car, Bundy took off in his Volkswagen bug and the officer gave chase. Bundy said his "paranoia" caused him to throw a bag of marijuana and cigarette papers out of a window during the several-blocks chase. He said he also left the window open to try to air out the car.

However, the officers who searched his car that night reported no tell-tale marijuana smell in the car or on Bundy and no signs he had been smoking pot.

Bundy contacted defense attorney John O'Connell August 22, but O'Connell did not learn what Bundy said was the real story until sometime after that Deputy County Attorney David Yocom heads the prosecution.

In other developments at the trial yesterday, former neighbors called by the state said Bundy did wear dark patent leather shoes and that his beige-colored Volkswagen bug had a long rip across the top of the back seat.

Carol DaRonch, 18, of suburban Murray, said her abductor the night of Nov. 8, 1974 wore such shoes and his Volkswagen bug had a seat rip.

Other neighbors called by the defense Thursday said Bundy never wore patent-leather shoes and that his auto did not have such a long rip in the back seat.

Yocom asked Bundy: "Did you tell Margerith Maughan (a Bundy acquaintance who testified Thursday) that I like virgins and can get them anytime?"

Bundy waving his hands, replied, "No."

Yocom then asked, "Did you tell her you felt there is no difference between right and wrong?"

Bundy said any such comments of his would have been "taken out of context... it does not represent my opinion on the subject." Bundy said that earlier on the night of August 15-16 he smoked a "joint" (marijuana cigarette) at home and checked a girlfriend's house but saw the lights were out as he drove by. He continued:

"So, I just decided, as is my habit, to drive around... I decided to explore an area I've never been in before." In the Granger residential area west of the Salt Lake City limits, he decided to smoke another "joint." He stopped and was smoking the cigarette when Utah State Patrol Sgt. Robert Hayward flicked his cruiser's bright lights on Bundy's unlighted auto.

Bundy said his paranoia caused him to take off. He explained he knew he was doing something illegal and that he was not going to get caught "with that stuff in my car." Hayward chased him several blocks before Bundy stopped at a service station.

The officers found an 18-inch crowbar a pair of handcuffs and items they described as burglar tools in Bundy's car. Bundy later also charged with attempting to evade an officer.

Bundy denied he abducted Ms. DaRonch from the Fashion Place Mall in Murray on Nov. 8, 1974. She had identified him as the man who, posing as a police officer, lured her into his auto, snapped handcuffs on one wrist, threatened to kill her with his small revolver and tried to strike her with a crowbar before she managed to escape.

Bundy said he didn't go to the Murray Mall that night. He said although it was difficult to reconstruct his activities that long ago, a record indicated he had some car trouble that afternoon and later "must have" gone home and had dinner. He then went to a movie in Salt Lake City, he said, later to a pub and "must have been home about 11:50 p.m."

A phone call was made from Bundy's apartment to Seattle, about that hour, records show.

Bundy's testimony indicated his Volkswagen was in rather poor running order at times in the fall of 1974. But Yocom produced gasoline credit slips of Bundy's showing that between Oct. 24 and 28, 1974, in four purchases Bundy bought 22 gallons of fuel.

It was stipulated this is enough gas to drive about 450 miles in the Volkswagen.

Yocom also produced slips indicating Bundy bought gasoline in Salt Lake City the day Ms. DaRonch was abducted. He cited other slips that indicated Bundy had been in Murray in late September and mid-October 1974.

Under Yocom's questioning, Bundy said he had been to the Fashion Place Mall. alone, in the fall of 1974. But he denied being there the night of the abduction. Yocom also showed that Bundy's gas slips for a time last year carried two different license plate numbers on the same car. Some slips showed the number of a plate Bundy had reported lost and for which he had obtained a replacement.

The defendant explained this by saying he must have given station attendants his old license plate number sometimes rather than the new one. Closing arguments are scheduled today before Third District Court Judge Stewart Hanson Jr., who is hearing the case without a jury.

February 28, 1976
Bundy Trial Winds Up

SALT LAKE CITY - The kidnaping case of Theodore R Bundy was taken under advisement yesterday following closing arguments by prosecution and defense.

There was no indication how long it would be before Judge Stewart Hanson Jr hands down his verdict on the case of the law student from Tacoma. Some courthouse sources said a month may not be too long for a judge to weigh such a case.

The trial ended after four days of testimony by 27 witnesses, including Carol DaRonch. The woman Bundy is accused of kidnaping Nov. 8, 1974, at a shopping mall in suburban Murray. In summations, Deputy County Attorney David Yocom argued that all the pieces of the crime fit Bundy "to a 'T'" and show he is guilty as charged.

Defense Attorney John O'Connell argued that the pieces of evidence could fit a number of other persons and that Bundy was a victim of mistaken identity by Ms DaRonch, who has identified him as her kidnaper.

Judge Hanson, in comments to counsel, said the case against Bundy will be decided solely "on the events of Nov. 8, 1974, and not on events of any other date."

He apparently was referring to other charges pending against Bundy, a one-time activist in Washington Republican politics.

March 2, 1976
Bundy Is Found Guilty
Jailed After Kidnap Verdict

SALT LAKE CITY - A Judge yesterday convicted Theodore R. Bundy of the aggravated kidnaping of a young woman here and sent the former Tacoma law student back to jail for his own protection.

Bundy, 29, former Republican Party aide in Washington State, showed no emotion at the verdict of Third District Court Judge Stewart Hanson Jr. But his mother, Mrs John Bundy, Tacoma, broke into sobs. Both parents were present during most of last week's five-day trial.

Sentencing was set for 9am March 22. The offense which Judge Hanson refused to reduce is punishable by five years to life imprisonment. Bundy could be given probation if the judge thought it warranted.

Notice of appeal is expected to be held soon, court sources said after which Bundy could ask for release on bail. Otherwise Judge Hanson remanded him to the Salt Lake County Jail here until sentencing. The judge freed Bundy's $15,000 bail to his attorney, John O'Connell.

The judge could not be reached for comment on putting Bundy back into jail "for his own protection." After the verdict, an aide said Judge Hanson was taking no calls. Courtroom security was tight when the verdict was given.

The judge deliberated the case over the weekend after the trial ended. Bundy had waived a jury trial.

Carol DaRonch, then 17 of suburban Murray, the kidnap victim identified Bundy during the trial as her abductor of Nov. 3, 1974. She had also identified him in a police lineup last Oct 2. When Bundy was charged with the crime, he spent eight weeks in jail before a $100,000 bond was reduced to $15,000 and posted.

Ms DaRonch, now 19, said Bundy posed as a policeman and said someone had tried to break into her auto at the Fashion Place shopping mall in Murray. The young woman said Bundy lured her into his tan Volkswagen Bug, drove a half-mile, then stopped.

He snapped handcuffs on one of her wrists threatened to "blow her head off" with a pistol then tried to strike her with a crowbar, the kidnap victim said. She fought and escaped.

Bundy, on the witness stand two hours Thursday, denied her claims. He and defense attorney John O'Connell said Bundy was a victim of misidentification by Ms DaRonch. University of Washington psychology Prof Elizabeth Loftus testified as a defense witness that eyewitness identifications often could be in error.

Bundy has been investigated by police in King County and in Utah and Colorado in connection with abductions and murders of a number of young women. While officers in the three states have said he is a suspect in those cases, no charges have resulted. The investigations are continuing.

Eight young women were abducted from this area in a six-month period in 1974 and remains of six were found last fall in the Issaquah area. A seventh skeleton could not be identified.

The only clue in those cases was a man who introduced himself as "Ted" seen leaving Lake Sammamish State Park July 14, 1974 with Jan Ott, 23, whose remains later were found near Issaquah. Denise Naslund, 18, also vanished from the park that day. Her remains were found with Ms Ott's.

Colorado authorities are investigating Bundy in connection with disappearances or murders of five young women in that state. Bodies of three have been found.

Utah authorities are probing the cases of five women who disappeared bodies of three have been found. In addition, several other Salt Lake City area women reported attempted kidnappings by a man during the fall months of 1974.

Bundy admitted on the witness stand Thursday that he lied to police and his attorney as to why he was in a Salt Lake City residential neighborhood at 2:30 am last Aug. 16 when first arrested by police.

He testified he was smoking marijuana and when a police car started following him, he "panicked" and tried to escape because he feared that getting "busted" for smoking pot could ruin his law career, so he said he lied by saying he'd been at a drive-in movie.

Deputy County Atty. David Yocom told the judge that he could distrust all of Bundy's testimony, due to the lie.

Bundy still faces charges of possessing burglary tools of trying to evade an officer and of false application for a duplicate vehicle title in Utah.

March 3, 1976
Bundy Case Stirs Probes In 3 States

Investigations into the disappearances or deaths of 18 young women in Washington, Utah and Colorado are being pushed. following the kidnaping conviction and jailing of Theodore Bundy in Salt Lake City, officers said yesterday.

They said Bundy, 29, of Tacoma, remains an active suspect in the tri-state cases.

He will be sentenced March 22 on the kidnaping conviction.

Authorities in the three states - including King County Pros. Atty. Christopher T. Bayley, expressed hope the conviction and jailing of Bundy "will encourage someone who may have knowledge of these cases to come forward."

In Aspen, Colo. Yesterday, Dist. Atty. Frank Tucker met with members of his staff and Pitkin County sheriff's officers to review evidence in the slaying of Caryn Campbell, a Michigan nurse, near Aspen last year.

Ms. Campbell vanished from a ski lodge Jan. 12, 1975. Her frozen body was found more than a month later along a remote road. Officers said she had been raped.

A member of Tucker's staff said officers have "evidence" in the case but he declined to say if it was something besides previously disclosed gasoline credit-card slips that indicated Bundy's auto had been in the Aspen area the same day Ms Campbell disappeared.

Den Dist. Atty Ashley Anderson said yesterday's conference should result in a decision on a course of action to be taken in Ms. Campbell's murder. Both Bayley and a Salt Lake County official said they hone Tucker's staff would "re-evaluate a decision not to file charges" in Ms Campbell's death, in light of the Bundy kidnaping conviction Monday.

Asked what this meant, Deputy Dist. Atty. Anderson said, "it wasn't our decision, it was a judge's," apparently indicating a judge thought officers had insufficient evidence to arrest anybody in the Campbell death.

Anderson said the situation would be given further scrutiny yesterday.

Officers of the three states met in Salt Lake City about a week before Bundy's trial there to again go over their respective evidence. They have had several such conferences.

Meanwhile, Bundy's attorney, John O'Connell, of Seattle said Judge Stewart Hanson Jr.'s conviction of Bundy on aggravated kidnaping charges Monday "shocked" both him and Bundy.

Contrary to outward appearances, O'Connell said Bundy "paled and could hardly walk" after hearing the decision "He was a mess," O'Connell said. "He was primarily concerned about his family."

Bundy's parents, Mr. and Mrs. John Bundy of Tacoma, sat throughout most of the trial and his mother sobbed at the decision.

O'Connell said he "assumes" Bundy's conviction will be appealed.

One of the missing Utah women is Debra Kent, 17, of Bountiful. just north of Salt Lake City. She vanished from a high school there Nov 8, 1974, the same night Carol DaRonch, 17, reported Bundy kidnaped her from a suburban Murray shopping mall.

Ms. DaRonch fought and escaped after the abductor snapped handcuffs on one of her wrists. Officers said a key found at the high school from which Ms Kent disappeared fit the handcuffs put on Ms. DaRonch's wrist.

March 4, 1976
New Evidence in Murder

New evidence given to Colorado authorities in a woman's murder is of a physical nature and recently was found in Salt Lake City area, a detective captain there said yesterday.

Salt Lake County sheriff's Capt. N. D. Hayward refused to detail the new evidence. It pertains to the death of Caryn Campbell, 24, a Michigan nurse who vanished Jan. 12 1975 from a ski lodge near Aspen, Colo. Her body was found Feb 18.

The new evidence was given to Pitkin County (Aspen) police prior to the aggravated kidnaping trial of Theodore R. Bundy, 29. in Salt Lake City. Hayward said Bundy was convicted and will be sentenced March 22.

March 23, 1976
Bundy Quizzed on Colorado Death

SALT LAKE CITY - The first Colorado authorities to question Theodore R. Bundy about murders in that state have interrogated the convicted kidnaper in the County Jail here, it was learned yesterday.

Also yesterday, the sentencing of Bundy, 29, for the Nov. 8, 1974 abduction of 17-year-old Carol DaRonch here was delayed 90 days so the former Tacoma resident can undergo a 90-day psychological evaluation at Utah State Prison.

Third District Court Judge Stewart M. Hanson Jr., who found Bundy guilty on March 1 of aggravated kidnaping, ordered the evaluations. Ile said the regular presentence report did not provide sufficient information for sentencing.

According to a sheriff's officer here, Pitkin County, Colo. Sheriff's Lt. William Baldridge and Michael Fisher, an investigator for that county's district attorney, questioned Bundy week ago in connection with the slaying of Caryn Campbell, 24, a Michigan nurse, near Aspen early last year.

The county officer said Bundy's attorney, John D. O'Connell, was present during the jail questioning and that the session was tape recorded. The officer added that he had little information on specifics of the questioning, except that it pertained to Ms. Campbell's murder.

The woman was on a skiing vacation near Aspen when she vanished Jan. 12, 1975. Her nude, frozen body was found in the area Feb. 18. She had been raped.

Since Bundy's arrest here last Oct. 2 on kidnaping charges, Colorado authorities have been endeavouring to question Bundy about several missing and murdered women in that state. Baldridge and Fisher were the first known officers to have succeeded.

Lawmen in this state and Washington have investigated Bundy in connection with abductions and the slayings of young women in the two states Colorado officers earlier had said gasoline credit card slips placed Bundy's auto in areas on the same dates three women, including Ms. Campbell, vanished.

The questioning of Bundy here by Colorado officers included queries about the credit card slips, the sheriff's office source said.

April 23, 1976
Bundy In Trial And Mistrial

SALT LAKE CITY - Convicted kidnaper Theodore Bundy went on trial - twice - yesterday on a misdemeanor charge of failure to stop for a police officer.

Third District Judge Gordon Hall began the trial during the morning with questioning of prospective jurors but granted a defense motion for a mistrial on grounds the questions revealed prejudicial material.

He began the trail again with a new group of jury candidates during the afternoon.

The judge asked prospective panelists about publicity concerning Bundy's kidnaping trial and the investigations by authorities in Utah, Colorado, and Washington into the kidnappings and slayings of several young women.

Bundy, 29, a University of Utah law student from Tacoma was convicted of aggravated kidnaping, March 1, following a nonjury trial.

The judge ordered a 90-day pre-sentence evaluation at Utah State Prison and has not yet sentenced Bundy for the abduction of Carol DaRonch of Murray, Utah, in the fall of 1974.

April 25, 1976
Another Conviction for Bundy

SALT LAKE CITY - Former University of Utah law student Theodore Bundy was convicted Friday of evading a police officer and was returned to the state prison where he is undergoing presentence evaluation on an aggravated kidnaping conviction.

A six-woman, two-man Salt Lake jury took 50 minutes to find Bundy guilty of the misdemeanor after a two-day trial. which had been delayed because publicity in the kidnaping case made jury selection difficult.

Bundy, 29, was convicted in the earlier case of abducting teenager Carol DaRonch from a suburban Salt Lake shopping center in November 1974. He also is being investigated in connection with abduction slayings in Utah. Colorado and Washington but has not been charged.

Bundy agreed to a sentencing date of June 22.

The misdemeanor charge carries a possible sentence of one year in the county jail and a $1000 fine. The aggravated kidnaping charge could carry five years, to life sentence.

Bundy testified earlier Friday he did not know it was an officer pursuing him through a suburban neighborhood last August.

Prosecutor Gary Pane asserted the prosecution proved there was a period of time when Bundy was evading police.

July 1, 1976
Bundy Gets 1 to 15 Years

Convicted kidnaper Theodore R. Bundy of Tacoma was sentenced in Salt Lake City to one to 15 years in prison yesterday for the abduction of a young woman in a Murray, Utah, shopping mall in 1974.

District Court Judge Stewart M. Hanson Jr. passed sentence after Bundy, a former University of Utah and University of Puget Sound law student, made a tearful plea that his incarceration would serve no purpose. "Yes, I will be a candidate for rehabilitation," Bundy said in court, "but not for what I have done, but what the system has done to me."

Bundy's attorney John D. O'- Connell told the P-1 he intends to file an appeal to the Utah State Supreme Court immediately. Bundy's fate is now up to the Utah Board of Pardons, which under ordinary circumstances might review a request for parole within six months of sentencing. Judge Hanson reduced the charge from a first degree to a second-degree count. A first-degree charge would have called for 5 years to life sentence. Hanson said he reduced the charge because there were no other instances of criminal charges of a similar nature against Bundy. After the kidnap sentencing. Bundy was taken to another courtroom before Judge Gordon Hall, who sentenced him to 60 days and a $250 fine on a conviction of evading a police officer. The fine was suspended, and the jail term made concurrent with the kidnaping term. The evasion of the police officer in August of 1975 led to Bundy's arrest in the kidnap case. Bundy appeared in Hanson's court as his own attorney for part of the proceedings and argued that his 90-day psychiatric evaluation at the Utah State Prison was inaccurate. Bundy objected to the psychiatric evaluation which described him as having an antisocial personality," "hostile" and being unable to handle stress. "He just underwent nine months of the worst stress I've seen, and he handled it better than Mr. Nixon handled Watergate, without breaking down," O'Connell told the P-I. Bundy also objected to the report's characterization of him as being "dependent on women." "Who isn't dependent on women?" he asked the judge.

Bundy, clad in jeans and a plaid shirt, argued for over an hour against basing his sentence on the evaluation. When he appeared in Hall's court immediately after the sentencing, he was chained around the waist and wearing an orange T-shirt with the word "diagnostic" pencilled on the back in black letters.

He was denied a request to speak with his mother before being returned to the penitentiary at Point of the Mountain in Draper.

"I thought he took it rather well," O'Connell said of Bundy after the sentencing. "I thought he made a rather eloquent speech on his own behalf. I think he showed that he could have been a good lawyer had this not happened."

Bundy's mother, father and brother were in the courtroom. and Mrs. Bundy came forward to comfort her son as he wept after his statement to the judge. She said, "We're not finished with this case. We're going to go on fighting it."

Bundy was convicted March 1 by Hanson on the kidnaping charge stemming from the Nov. 1974 abduction of Carol DaRonch, 19. She said Bundy posed as 2 policemen, got her into his car, handcuffed her. and threatened her with a Crowbar. She said she leaped from his car shortly after leaving the mall and was picked up by a passing motorist.

The kidnaping of Miss DaRonch came during a series of Utah-area abductions of young women, some of whom were found slain.

Bundy was investigated by police in connection with slayings of young women in this state and Colorado, but no charges have been filed in these cases.

When he was arrested for evading the policeman. officers found handcuffs and a crowbar in his car. Bundy said on the stand that he had lied to policemen about his reason for being in the Granger suburb in the middle of the night and tried to escape because he had been smoking marijuana. He initially told police he had been to a movie.

Bundy, 29, is a graduate of the University of Washington and was a political worker on Gov. Dan Evan's campaign in 1972.

Bundy, who has spent the last 10 months in jail, told the judge before sentencing: "Someday, who knows when, 5 to 10 years in the future, when the times come when I can leave, I suggest you ask yourself where we are, what's been accomplished, was the sacrifice of my life worth it all?"

October 23, 1976
Murder Warrant Served on Bundy

SALT LAKE CITY - Convicted kidnaper Theodore R. Bundy was served at the Utah State Prison yesterday with a warrant of arrest for the murder of a young Michigan nurse near Aspen, Colo., last year.

Bundy, 29, former resident of Tacoma and University of Washington law student, has been investigated in connection with the deaths of about a dozen young women in the Pacific North-west, Utah and Colorado.

Although he was convicted of kidnaping a 17-year-old girl in a Salt Lake suburb, he has never previously been charged with murder.

In Aspen, Dist. Atty. Frank Tucker said he had begun extradition proceedings to return Bundy to Colorado "for the purpose of prosecuting Bundy for first-degree murder in connection with the death of Caryn Campbell."

Miss Campbell, 24, a Dearborn, Mich., nurse, was visiting Aspen on a skiing vacation with her fiancé in January 1975, when she disappeared. Her nude body was found the following month under a snowbank on a rural road leading to the ski resort.

Pitkin County officers in Colorado have said credit card slips signed by Bundy in Aspen on Jan. 12, the day Miss Campbell disappeared, have been found by investigators.

The district attorney's office would not reveal what other evidence lawmen might have against Bundy in connection with the death of Miss Campbell.

The arrest warrant was served on Bundy in the maximum-security area of the prison where he is serving a sentence of one to 15 years for the aggravated kidnaping of Carol DaRonch at a shopping mall in 1974.

The young woman escaped from her abductor, and later picked Bundy out of a police lineup.

David Yacom, deputy Salt Lake County attorney, Pitkin County investigator Michael Fisher and a Salt Lake County deputy went to the prison to serve the arrest warrant.

Bruce Lebeck, law partner of John O'Connell, Bundy's Salt Lake attorney, was present when the warrant was served. O'Connell was in court at the time.

Yacom, who successfully prosecuted Bundy on the kidnaping charge, said the next step is for Salt Lake County to file a fugitive complaint on which Bundy probably will be arraigned Tuesday in City Court.

Yacom described that complaint as the first step in extradition proceedings that he believes will eventually lead to Bundy's return to Colorado and trial in Aspen.

However, if Bundy fights extradition, the process could take "considerable time," Yacom said.

Bundy was investigated, along with more than 2,800 other persons, in connection with the "Ted murders" of college-age girls in Washington and Oregon. Witnesses in some of these cases told officers that a person who identified himself as "Ted" was seen with the victim just before she disappeared.

Bundy has never been charged in connection with any of these cases.

Bundy's attorney, John O'Connell, was critical yesterday of the manner in which the arrest warrant had been served on Bundy in prison.

He said the accused man's attorney had not been notified in advance. When he got out of court, he said, he learned that his law partner, Lebeck, had rushed to the prison on short notice.

"Authorities call the news media first and the lawyers second," he said. "This case is being tried in the newspapers."

Bundy was a law student at the University of Utah when he was arrested on the kidnaping charge. He moved there from Seattle where he attended the UW.

October 26, 1977
New Move On Bundy By Utah Prosecutor

Colo. - Special Prosecutor Milton Blakey has filed sealed evidence he claims links former Tacoman Theodore Bundy with a slaying and the disappearance of two 17-year-old girls in Utah in 1974. District Court Judge George Lohr will hear arguments Nov 2.

The filing by Blakey is part of the legal maneuvering preliminary to Bundy's trial for the January 1975, slaying of a Michigan nurse, Caryn Campbell. Miss Campbell was vacationing at Snow. mass near Aspen when she was slain.

Blakey filed a notice of intent Sept. 7 that he will try to link Bundy with the murder of Laura Ann Aime of Salem, Utah, whose body was found Nov. 27, 1974. after she was missing a week. The prosecutor said he also would try to show that Bundy was involved in the disappearance of Debra Kent from a parking lot near Viewmont High School in Bountiful, Utah, in 1974 Bundy, who is defending himself, said there is no connection among the cases. Lohr gave both sides a week to submit briefs, prior to the Nov 2 date.

October 27, 1976
Bundy Arraigned in Utah On Fugitive Charges

Convicted kidnaper Theodore Bundy was arraigned yesterday in Salt Lake City on charges of being a fugitive from Colorado where he is wanted for first-degree murder in the death of a Michigan nurse.

Bundy's attorney, John D. O'Connell, said he did not know the purpose of issuing the fugitive warrant since the former Tacoma resident already is in the Utah State Prison. City Judge Melvin Morris read the warrant to the 29-year-old former law student who has been questioned by authorities about the deaths or disappearances of 18 young women in four Western states including Washington.

Authorities said issuance of the warrant was a preliminary step in the extradition of Bundy, who is now serving a 1-to-15-year sentence in prison for the abduction of a teen-aged girl from a suburban shopping mall near Salt Lake. She escaped and later identified Bundy as her abductor.

David Yocum, deputy Salt Lake County attorney, said Pitkin County, Colo. officials next must seek a governor's warrant within a 30-day period, asking Bundy be transferred to Colorado to be tried in the death of Caryn Campbell, 23, who disappeared Jan. 12. 1975 while on skiing vacation with her fiancé at Aspen, Colo.

Bundy's lawyer charged the new legal action against Bundy was "filed to help get the Pitkin County attorney re-elected." Yesterday's hearing was manufactured as a media event, O'Connell said.

O'Connell claimed Colorado authorities could have initiated extradition proceedings without hand-delivering a warrant to Bundy in prison last Friday and without having local fugitive charges filed. Bundy issued a statement following the arraignment saying he was confident he would be cleared "should I be allowed a fair trial in Colorado" and of the kidnaping conviction on appeal.

"I have never killed, never kidnaped and never even desired to injure another human being," Bundy said. "I am prepared to use every ounce of strength I have to vindicate myself. I am prepared to overcome the massive and prejudicial publicity which significantly affected my first trial and promises to influence the second." He concluded that he would win "because I am right."

October 29, 1976
Bundy Escape Try Suspected

Theodore Bundy, convicted of kidnaping in Utah and charged with murder in Colorado, apparently planned to escape from Utah State Penitentiary, Warden Samuel Smith said yesterday.

Bundy, 29, from Tacoma and Seattle, who has been investigated in the disappearances or deaths of 18 young women in this state and Utah and Colorado, was found with an apparent "escape kit" October 19. Smith said,

The warden said materials found on Bundy that "indicated he might be planning to travel" included road maps. a Social Security card with another's name on it, a sketch of a driver's license and scribbled notes on airline schedules.

Smith was unable to say how Bundy explained the items, if he did. The warden said Bundy, serving 1-15 years for kidnaping a suburban Salt Lake City young woman in 1974, worked in the prison print shop, where he may have made the Social Security card and planned to print the driver's license, which Smith said was for a Midwestern state.

"He was either planning to escape or to assist someone else to escape," Smith said. He said another inmate suspected of helping put the escape kit together later was cleared.

Bundy was given 15 days in isolation by a hearing board that investigated the escape kit matter. He still is in isolation. Smith said a prison board also is considering whether to change Bundy's custody classification from medium to maximum security.

While the apparent escape plan was uncovered before Colorado authorities recently served a murder warrant charging Bundy with slaying Caryn Campbell, 24, a Michigan nurse, near Aspen, Jan. 12, 1975, newspapers and wire services earlier had reported that Colorado was seeking the murder charge against the prisoner.

Smith said he had no knowledge if the Colorado 'case and the apparent escape plan were connected. Colorado has started extradition proceedings against Bundy.

Bundy was arraigned in a Salt Lake City court last Monday on charges of being a fugitive from Colorado, a first step in extradition.

The prison, at Point-of-the-Mountain, is 20 miles south of Salt Lake City.

Smith said a print shop supervisor suspected Bundy was "putting together an escape kit" and that when the prisoner was shaken down coming out of the industrial area, some of the materials were found on him.

Asked how a prisoner might plan to escape the penitentiary, Smith said:

"We have trucks that go in and out of the industrial area regularly-but I would have no idea if this was planned."

Smith said Bundy had been a good prisoner who got along well with fellow inmates.

Bundy was a suspect in the deaths of several young women from this area and in the disappearances and deaths of other women in Utah and Colorado. Colorado officers say they have physical evidence against Bundy in Ms. Campbell's death but Utah and Washington authorities have said they haven't uncovered any such evidence in their cases.

November 24, 1976
Bundy Extradition Papers

Extradition papers from Colorado have been received by the Utah governor's office for convicted kidnaper Theodore Bundy, 29. Colorado authorities have filed first-degree murder charges against the former University of Utah law student, accusing him of slaying Caryn Campbell, Campbell, 23, a nurse from Dearborn, Mich., who disappeared Jan. 12, 1975, while on a skiing vacation at Aspen.

Bundy, serving one to fifteen years in Utah for the abduction of a 17-year-old girl, has been held in maximum security since escape materials were found in his possession last month.

"I am prepared to use every ounce of strength I have to vindicate myself," Bundy said.

December 17, 1976
Bundy Still Fights Extradition

Theodore R. Bundy of Tacoma, now serving time in Utah for kidnaping, continued yesterday to fight extradition to Colorado. where he faces a first-degree murder charge.

Attorneys for Bundy filed a writ in Salt Lake City district court charging the Colorado warrant does not comply with the law and does not provide enough information about the murder charge the court will hear arguments on the writ January 27.

Bundy, who has been investigated for the disappearances of young women in Utah and Washington. is wanted in Colorado in connection with the death of a Michigan nurse, Caryn Campbell.

January 29, 1977
Transfer Fight Dropped by Bundy

Theodore R. Bundy has dropped his fight against extradition from. Utah to Colorado, where he will stand trial for first-degree murder in the Jan. 12, 1975 sex- slaying of Michigan nurse Caryn Campbell, 23, near an Aspen area ski lodge. Bundy, 30, a convicted kidnaper serving 1-15 years in the Utah State Prison, will be moved to the Pitkin County jail in Aspen by Monday, authorities said.

He is expected to be held there until his trial begins, possibly some- time in the late spring or early summer, an assistant district attorney in Aspen said.

Bundy formerly lived in Tacoma and Seattle and was on former Gov. Dan Evans' 1972 campaign staff.

He was convicted last March in Salt Lake City of kidnaping Carol DaRonch, then 17. from a suburban shopping center Nov. 8, 1974.

In a statement at a scheduled extradition hearing in Salt Lake City yesterday Bundy said he dropped his challenge to extradition because "I am certain I will be acquitted in Colorado." Ms. Campbell's nude, frozen body was found. six weeks after her disappearance several miles from the lodge. She had been raped and bludgeoned, officers said.

February 6, 1977
Bundy - The Colorado Murder Case

Friends and fellow workers used such superlatives as "Young Mr. America" and "Mr. Young Republican" in describing Theodore R. Bundy.

Personable, helpful, handsome, smart, and kind. A young man who took up law, thinking it important to the political career he cherished. He knew high people in the state Republican Party here and campaigned for several, including former Gov. Dan Evans.

By most measurements, Ted Bundy, who seemed sort of an American ideal, was destined to be a winner.

Those holding him in such high esteem were confounded when Bundy, of Tacoma and Seattle, became a suspect in disappearances and deaths of about 20 young women in King County, Utah, and Colorado.

Now Bundy, who has turned 30, has left the Utah State Prison maximum security cell he has occupied as a convicted kidnaper and is in Colorado to stand trial for first-degree murder.

But for his friends, there is something even worse.

Like Gary Gilmore, a loser who got his death wish before a firing squad in the same Utah prison, Ted Bundy could face execution in Colorado's gas chamber if convicted of the charge against him in that state.

Colorado has the death penalty and first-degree murder is a capital offense there. The state has four men on death row at the state prison in Canyon City, 110 miles southwest of Denver.

The newest man on Colorado's death row was sent there just recently for killing his wife.

The jury or judge deciding a murder case in Colorado can decide whether to impose the death penalty under the state's capital punishment statute, enacted in 1975.

Michael Fisher, of the district attorney's office in Aspen, said Colorado was the last state to execute someone for murder, in 1967, prior to Gilmore's recent firing squad death in Utah. The U.S. Supreme Court banned capital punishment after that but now has allowed it to resume.

Although Bundy could face execution if convicted of first-degree murder in Colorado, the appeal process and the continuing controversy over reinstitution of the death penalty undoubtedly would delay considerably that grim possibility.

Colorado Gov. Richard Lamm opposed capital punishment while in the state legislature - and he has the power to commute the death penalty to life imprisonment, although he has not indicated he plans to do so in the case of the four now on death row there.

Bundy is charged in the Jan. 12, 1975 sex-slaying of Caryn Campbell, 23, a Dearborn, Mich., nurse, whose nude, frozen body was found near Aspen six weeks after she vanished from outside Wildwood Lodge, between Aspen and Snowmass.

She had accompanied her fiancé, a doctor, to Colorado for a medical convention at the lodge and also was on a skiing holiday. She vanished after going from dinner at the lodge to her room. When her body was found on February 18, it was determined she had been raped. She had been bludgeoned to death.

Colorado officers say they have evidence, for use at the trial in Aspen, that Bundy was in the area the day Ms. Campbell disappeared from the lodge.

The evidence includes a Chevron credit card, issued to Bundy, which was used in the Aspen area that day. The Pitkin County district attorney's office also is reported to be counting on at least one eyewitness identification of Bundy "in the lodge area" around the time of Ms. Campbell's disappearance. The reported eyewitness is a woman who has given a statement to authorities.

Other evidence includes scalp hair that the prosecution will contend came from Ms. Campbell, that has been analyzed by the FBI crime laboratory.

Salt Lake County, Utah, sheriff's officers said they found the hair samples on the front floor of Bundy's Volkswagen bug when they vacuumed the auto after Bundy's first arrest in Salt Lake City on Aug. 16, 1975.

The FBI lab also reported that pubic hair found in the trunk of the Volkswagen matches that of Melissa Smith, 17, slain near Salt Lake City in the fall of 1974. Her father is police chief of suburban Midvale.

Officers say the FBI lab report on the hair samples doesn't prove the hair came from the two victims but rather that it matches their hair in constitution.

The hair believed from the Smith girl could mean more trouble for Bundy in Utah, where he was convicted last March of kidnaping a girl, 17, from a suburban Salt Lake City shopping center.

She managed to escape, and it was principally her eyewitness identification of him as her abductor that sent Bundy to the Utah prison for 1-15 years.

Capt. N.D: (Pete) Hayward, detective chief in Salt Lake County, said Bundy remains a major suspect in at least four disappearances and deaths of young women in that area in the fall of 1974, including Ms. Smith.

Asked if the hair samples believed to be from Ms. Smith could result in Utah also charging Bundy with murder, Hayward said:

"That case is very much alive, as are our investigations into the others."

Bundy also remains a prime suspect in the disappearances and deaths of eight young women in King County during the first half of 1974. Sparse remains of six of them were later found at two sites near Issaquah.

Capt. Nick Mackie, chief of King County detectives, said his office has not dropped its investigation of Bundy as the prime suspect in these cases. But his Utah kidnaping conviction and the Colorado murder charge have pushed the local investigation into the background.

"Our trail is the coldest in the three states," Mackie explained. "If we had found enough evidence, we most certainly would have filed charges in our cases."

The vacuuming of Bundy's bug in Salt Lake City produced no hair samples that matched those of the King County victims, a King County officer said.

Bundy's name was turned in to the sheriff's office here not too long after a mysterious "Ted" was seen at Lake Sammamish State Park on July 14, 1974. "Ted" approached several women, asking for help in loading a sailboat atop his Volkswagen bug. He wore one arm in a sling and was seen leaving the park with Janice Ott, 23.

Later the same day, Denise Naslund, 18, vanished from the park. The remains of the two women were found Sept. 7, 1974, near Issaquah and the remains of four or five other missing women were found at a site 10 miles away later that fall.

"Ted's" appearance that day triggered a massive task force investigation into the cases of the missing women - but the probe went nowhere, until Bundy's first arrest, Aug. 16, 1975, in Salt Lake City.

Bundy then became a prime suspect in the King County cases.

Although members of the city-county task force questioned many "suspects" and investigated about 3,000 in all, as well as 1,100 vehicles - Bundy has never been questioned by local authorities.

Both Utah and Colorado officers succeeded in questioning Bundy extensively but Mackie, who headed the local task force, said when King County detectives first tried to see the suspect in Utah, Bundy's attorney refused to allow the interview.

A second effort was made, with similar results, Mackie said. Bundy's kidnapping charge and trial in Utah and now the Colorado murder charge against him apparently have precluded for the present any further attempts by King County officers to interrogate Bundy about the eight missing or dead women in King County, including Janice Ott and Denise Naslund.

Asked why Bundy wasn't questioned when his name was turned in (the person who did it said Bundy resembled composite drawings of "Ted" carried by newspapers), Mackie replied:

"He didn't look that good then... a lot of others looked better."

But he emphasized that the cases her are not closed. He also noted that the strategy of authorities in the three states as to seek convictions in cases where the best evidence was available. When Bundy left here in the fall of 1974 to study law at the University of Utah, local officers alerted Utah police.

"There has been a complete exchange of information on all the cases among officers of the three states," Mackie said.

California slayings at first believed possibly connected to those in the other three states have been eliminated, he added.

If Bundy's image to his friends was that of "Young Mr. America," a psychiatric evaluation of him at Utah state prison strongly contradicts that impression.

The evaluation found that Bundy:

"Is dependent on women, has an "anti-social personality," harbors "passive aggressiveness," and is a "private person."

Friends and fellow workers have a hard time matching that description with the Ted Bundy they remember. Bundy himself took issue with the evaluation process, saying he wasn't treated like others who were under diagnosis.

He has steadfastly proclaimed his innocence of all charges and suspicions and has his kidnaping conviction under appeal. Bundy says he knows he will win because "I am right."

But during his kidnaping trial, he admitted he lied to both police and his own attorney. Assistant Salt Lake County Atty. David Yocom, prosecuting Bundy, told Judge Stewart Hanson Jr., this meant all of Bundy's testimony, including his denials, could be disregarded.

Judge Hanson, to some extent anyway, agreed because in convicting Bundy of the kidnaping, he rejected the defendant's sworn testimony that he had not kidnaped the girl, Carol DaRonch, who said Bundy tried to kill her.

One of Bundy's attorneys at his kidnaping trial was Bruce C. Lubeck, who saw Bundy every week at the Utah prison. Lubeck says Bundy, who has had two years of law school at the University of Puget Sound and at the University of Utah, is helping prepare his own defense to the Colorado murder charge. He says he is "certain of acquittal."

Pitkin County, Colo., officers report that a public defender has been named to help defend Bundy in Aspen. It is unknown whether Bundy will have a private attorney on the case.

While Bundy said he is confident of acquittal in the Colorado case, he apparently attempted to escape the Utah prison just before the Colorado murder charge was served on him last October. Warden Sam Smith said, "Bundy was planning to travel or to help someone who was." Fake identification and other documents were found on Bundy, Smith said. This led to his being moved from medium to maximum security.

Bundy's transfer to Aspen from the Utah prison takes the suspect from one publicity-bathed spot to another.

The Utah prison, 20 miles south of Salt Lake City, got a great deal of publicity over Gilmore's recent execution.

Aspen, where Bundy will go on trial for murder in the spring or summer, held the glare of publicity during the recent trial of showgirl Claudine Longet in the accidental shooting death of her lover, pro skier Vladimir "Spider" Sabich.

Bundy has had plenty of publicity, too – and he blames it for much of his troubles, particularly the kidnaping conviction. But

Judge Hanson rejected that contention, saying publicity about the case was not a factor in his convicting Bundy.

John D. O'Connell, chief defense attorney in that trial, said the press made Bundy out to be a "monster" because he is suspected in the chain of deaths in the three states.

Bundy's friends have great difficulty matching the "American ideal" they remember with the "monster" image cited by O'Connell.

February 11, 1977
Bundy Files Here Studied

Pitkin County, Colo., District Attorney Frank G. E. Tucker is in Seattle to compare notes on Theodore R. Bundy, one of many suspects investigated, but not charged, in connection with the mysterious "Ted murders" of Seattle-area women in 1973 and 1974.

Tucker said yesterday he was meeting with Seattle and King County police "to go over their files to see if there may be something of interest to me… which relates to Mr. Bundy." A former Seattle resident, Bundy is charged with first-degree murder in the death of Caryn Campbell, 23, a Michigan nurse who disappeared from an Aspen, Colo. ski resort in January 1975.

Bundy was extradited to Colorado last month from Utah, where he was serving a prison term for second-degree kidnaping in the abduction of a young woman in Salt Lake City.

April 5, 1977
Witness Cannot Identify Bundy

At a preliminary hearing yesterday in Aspen, Colo., a California woman was unable to identify Theodore Bundy as one of the men she saw near a ski lodge elevator the night a Michigan nurse disappeared. Bundy, a former resident of Washington State, is charged with the murder of the nurse, Caryn Campbell. The witness, Elizabeth Harder said, "I'm just not sure of everything" and I just can't remember." She said she had trouble remembering details of the men and that "the light was poor that night."

She could not pick Bundy's picture from a group of seven handed. her by a prosecutor. Asked if anyone in the room looked familiar, she pointed to an under- sheriff. Authorities said she had earlier tentatively identified Bundy. Miss Campbell and her fiancé, Dr. Raymond Gadowski of Dearborn, Mich. had taken a ski vacation in Aspen in 1975. Gadowski described their day and an incident in which she became annoyed when he would not go to her room and get a magazine. She went to get the magazine herself. Her body was found in a snowbank a month later. Bundy was convicted of aggravated kidnaping last year in Salt Lake City.

April 6, 1977
FBI Aide Says Hair Found in Bundy Car

ASPEN Colo. - An FBI official testified yesterday strands of hair found in Theodore Bundy's car matched those of a Michigan nurse kidnaped from a ski lodge, and later slain, while vacationing with her fiancé.

Robert Neill said laboratory tests also showed additional hair found in Bundy's car matched those of women he had tried to abduct and Melissa Smith, 17, beaten and killed by her kidnaper in October 1974.

Neill testified on the second day of Bundy's preliminary hearing on charges stemming from the kidnaping and death of Caryn Campbell, of Dearborn, Mich. in January 1975. Bundy, a former resident of Washington State, currently is serving 1-15 years in the Utah state prison for the attempted abduction of Carol DaRonch from a shopping mall parking lot.

District Judge George Lohr said he would decide today whether to order Bundy bound over to District Court on charges stemming from Miss Campbell's slaying. Bundy has not been charged in Miss Smith's death.

Neill also said Bundy used credit cards to purchase gasoline at nearby Glenwood Springs, Colo., The week Miss Campbell disappeared and said a map found in Bundy's apartment in Utah had the town of Aspen circled.

Miss Campbell vanished from her resort lodge, also circled on the map, after leaving her fiancé and going to her room to get a magazine. Her body was found one month later beneath a snowbank on a road leading into town.

April 7, 1977
Judge Rules Bundy Be Tried in Murder

ASPEN, Colo. - District Court Judge George E. Lohr ruled yesterday Theodore R. Bundy should stand trial on a first-degree murder charge in the death two years ago of a Michigan nurse.

Lohr had no comment on the case, except to say he had reviewed the evidence presented at a preliminary hearing Monday and Tuesday.

A hearing on motions is set for May 6. No trial date has been set.

Bundy is accused of the January 1975 slaying of Caryn Campbell, a Dearborn, Mich. nurse who was vacationing in Aspen when she disappeared. Her nude, frozen body was found a month later beside a rural road.

Bundy, 29, a former Washington State Republican Party worker, was extradited from Utah, where he was serving a 1-to-15-year sentence for the 1974 kidnaping of a Salt Lake City girl.

An FBI agent testified Tuesday that hair substances found in Bundy's car were of the same type as those of Miss Campbell.

April 13, 1977
Bundy Transferred

Theodore Bundy, a former Tacoman awaiting trial in Aspen, Colo., for the 1975 slaying of a Michigan nurse, was transferred to the Garfield County Jail, about 45 miles away, "for health reasons and his own safety."

The Colorado Health Department had ordered that no prisoner be held in the Pitkin County Jail for more than 30 days because of inadequate space and lighting.

Bundy had opposed the transfer. He was ordered last week to stand trial for the January 1975, slaying of Caryn Campbell, 23, a Dearborn, Mich., nurse vacationing near Aspen.

May 13, 1977
Bundy Protests Conditions

Theodore Bundy, a former Washington resident charged with murder, has filed a motion in U.S. District Court in Aspen, Colo. protesting what he calls "harsh and unwarranted" treatment in his Colorado jail cell. The 30-year-old former law student, acting as his own attorney. complained about conditions at Garfield County Jail in Glenwood Springs. In his motion. he claims to have been held in a solitary cell under maximum-security isolation for one month. Bundy's motion said he slept on a plastic mattress with a hard, dirty blanket and no sheets or pillowcases. He said the air in his cell was "hot and stagnant," causing eye irritation and skin dryness. He also complained that he received no lunch.

May 18, 1977
Bundy Convinced of Innocence

SALT LAKE CITY - Convicted kidnaper Theodore Bundy, a former Seattle and Tacoma resident accused of killing a Michigan woman in Colorado. says he is convinced "more than ever" of his innocence.

Bundy, a former Washington State Republican Party aide and Utah law student, is preparing his own defense. He has been investigated in connection with murders of young women in several Western states but has been charged in only one.

"By putting myself in the position of being my own counsel, I'm using positive psychology. I'm going to do it. I'm going to do it because I'm right, because the person I'm representing is innocent," Bundy said in an interview at the Garfield County Jail in Colorado by a Salt Lake City television reporter.

Bundy, 30, is charged with killing Caryn Campbell, 24. Dearborn, Mich., whose nude and frozen body was found five days after she disappeared near Aspen in January 1975. He is expected to stand trial on the charge sometime in the fall.

Bundy was convicted in March 1976 of second-degree kidnaping in the abduction of a Utah girl who identified him in court. He was sentenced to 1-15 years in Utah State Prison.

He was extradited to Colorado in the Campbell case last January.

Bundy told reporter Barbara Grossman: "I wanted to get involved because I'm such a part of the defense. After all, I'm going to bear the consequences. Why not bear the responsibility of seeking my own acquittal and sustaining my own innocence?"

Bundy said he was confident he would be found innocent. He stays in a 6-by-12-foot cell at the Garfield jail in Glenwood Springs. His trial is to be in Aspen. Authorities say he is kept from contact with other jail inmates but is allowed to use the county law library.

Asked how he keeps his sanity. Bundy said, "I had a year's training course in Utah," referring to his year in prison.

'I had a lot of time to work on it," he said. "It wasn't easy at first. Now it is. They've made me hard. I can spend time in there (his cell). I don't like it. I'll never accept it. But I can deal with it, because I know how to create my own environment in my head. I don't look at the ceiling or the walls. 1 don't anguish over the fact I've lost my freedom."

May 29, 1977
Bundy Trial Date Set In Aspen

ASPEN, Colo. - Theodore Bundy's first-degree murder trial in the 1975 slaying of Caryn Campbell, a vacationing Michigan nurse, is set for November 14 here.

Bundy, 30, formerly of Tacoma and Seattle, is being held in Garfield County Jail, about 40 miles from Aspen. He is preparing his defense and will represent himself at the trial.

Bundy has asked that the death penalty be waived and that the press be barred from the trial. A judge will rule on the two motions in June.

Bundy was extradited to Colorado from Utah. where he was serving a term after being convicted of kidnaping a young woman at a Salt Lake City suburb.

June 8, 1977
Colorado Escape
Manhunt for Bundy

ASPEN, Colo. - The biggest manhunt in this mining and skiing town's history resumes at first light today for Theodore R. Bundy, murder suspect and convicted kidnaper, who leaped to freedom yesterday from a second-story courthouse window.

He was being sought last night by more than 150 law officers and volunteers in six counties.

"This is an extremely dangerous man we're dealing with," Pitkin County Undersheriff Ben Myers said. "Very dangerous."

At the request of Pitkin County Sheriff Dick Kienast, no guns were being sold in the area yesterday, and Kienast said he was worried the fugitive might take hostages.

"Any man desperate enough to jump 25 feet and risk broken logs or ankles is dangerous," the sheriff said of Bundy, who is a prime suspect in the disappearances and deaths of 18 women in Colorado, Utah and Washington State.

The sheriff noted that Bundy, charged with the 1975 murder of a woman near here and convicted of kidnapping a girl near Salt Lake City, tried to escape from the Utah state prison last October.

More than 200 searchers, divided into numerous possess, were to fan out into the hills at dawn today to join the manhunt. They were to be aided by six tracking dogs and a helicopter.

Bundy, 30, a onetime University of Washington student formerly of Tacoma and Seattle, leaped out the window of the old red-brick Pitkin County courthouse about 10:15 a.m. yesterday during a recess in a court hearing in his murder case.

He left footprints in the lawn three inches deep and was seen running down an alley minutes later. Other reports had him running down Main Street and running across a woman's lawn east of town. Dogs tracked him to the Roaring Fork River about a quarter mile east of downtown Aspen but lost the scent there.

Some officers believe Bundy crossed or at least went into the river and then doubled back and perhaps holed up in a vacant house for the night.

Houses were being checked in the darkness. A steady, cold rain set in last evening, promising to wipe out Bundy's trail for the dogs.

Roadblocks were set up on all main roads out of town. Dogs were called in, some by airplane from Denver. A helicopter was sent aloft.

All available deputies joined in, as did about 20 sheriff's reservists, Aspen police, the U.S. Forest Service and the Rocky Mountain U.S. Rescue Squad.

Parents were contacted to make sure they were home before children were sent home from school. Adult guards were posted on school buses. Long lines of automobiles with out-of-state license plates were backed up at police roadblocks as tourists fled town.

Bundy has been in Colorado since January, after being extradited from Utah where he had been convicted in March 1976 of kidnaping a young woman in a Salt Lake City suburb. He is serving a one-to-15-year sentence for the Utah conviction.

Yesterday, Bundy was in District Court Judge George Lohr's courtroom for a pretrial hearing on a charge that he murdered a Michigan nurse, Caryn Campbell, 23, near Aspen. Her nude, frozen body was discovered six weeks after she disappeared on Jan. 12, 1975, from outside a ski resort near here.

The hearing was on Bundy's motions to strike the death penalty, should he be convicted of the murder, and for a bill of particulars. The trial is scheduled for November 14.

During a recess, Bundy, who planned to represent himself at the trial (he was a law student at the University of Puget Sound in Tacoma and later at the University of Utah), walked alone to a small law library in the back of the courtroom, ostensibly to check law books.

A court official said the library is partially partitioned off from the courtroom by a shoulder-high shelf of books. It was through one of the open windows in the library that Bundy leaped.

Whitney Wulff, secretary to Sheriff Kienast, said Bundy's handcuffs had been removed for the court appearance. He was wearing a brown ensemble at the time of his escape, she said, including loafers, corduroy pants and a turtleneck sweater.

A passing citizen alerted the sheriff's office to the escape.

The unidentified man rushed into the sheriff's office in the courthouse and said: "I just saw a man jump out of a second-story window. Is that normal?"

Wulff said the sheriff's staff looked at one another and she cried out: "Bundy!"

Near Bundy's footprints below the escape window, Wulff said, she found legal papers the prisoner had been carrying. Someone else found a tan-and-white sweater Bundy had been wearing.

Sheriff Kienast said that at the time Bundy jumped out of the window, the single deputy who escorted the prisoner to the courtroom was outside in the hall, watching the door.

Asked if he viewed that as a lapse in the deputy's performance of his duties, Kienast said, "No."

The Caryn Campbell murder for which Bundy is scheduled to stand trial is the only slaying with which he has been charged.

And Maj. Nick Mackie, chief of King County detectives, pointed out yesterday that while Bundy is a suspect in the deaths and disappearances that shook Western Washington three years ago, no charges have been filled against him. Mackie said there is not enough evidence "to get past a preliminary hearing."

Of all the cases where Bundy is a suspect, Mackie said, "we've got the coldest trail." Bones of six of the young women believed murdered in King County have been found, and that is not even enough to disclose the cause of death. No trace has been found of the other two young women who disappeared.

The suspect in the cases here was known as "Ted" because that is the name he reportedly used when approaching several young women at Lake Sammamish State Park on July 14, 1974, before being seen leaving the park with a woman whose bones were found near Issaquah two months later.

Utah prison authorities believed Bundy was planning to escape from the state penitentiary there. Last October they said he was found in possession of road maps, a Social Security card with a false name, a sketch of a driver's license and notes on airline schedules.

He served 15 days in solitary and then was transferred to maximum security as a result.

Since April, when he was transferred from the Pitkin County jail because the state health department said the jail has inadequate lighting and space and because it affords poor security, Bundy has been held in the Garfield County jail in Glenwood Springs, about 35 miles northwest of Aspen.

Bundy has been transported to Aspen "about once a week for the past several weeks" to argue motions in his case, the sheriff's secretary said.

He had studied law at the University of Puget Sound and University of Utah but had not received his degree.

Nevertheless, he was acting as his own attorney in the murder case because, he told a reporter last month, "I'm using positive psychology, I'm going to do it because I'm right, because the person I'm representing is innocent.

"Why not hear the responsibility of seeking my own acquittal and sustaining my own innocence?"

The motion being argued in District Court Judge George Lohr's courtroom yesterday was one made by Bundy seeking to have the death-penalty option removed from the jury should he be convicted of Campbell's murder.

June 9, 1977
Sheriff Says: We Goofed on Bundy

ASPEN, Colo. - Sheriff Dick Kienast admitted yesterday that "we screwed up" in allowing murder suspect Ted Bundy to escape Tuesday by leaping 25 feet from a second-story window of the Pitkin County courthouse here.

Bundy was still at large last night. "I feel (bleepy) about it," said the jeans-clad sheriff.

He said the single officer guarding Bundy at a court hearing should have been close to the prisoner, rather than out in the hall watching the doorway.

Kienast said that while the officer kept an eye on the door Bundy bailed out the window.

The sheriff identified the lone guard as Deputy David Westerlund, who was not available for questions.

Bundy, alone, walked to a small law library at the rear of the courtroom and screened by shoulder-high bookshelves, made his leap to freedom. He escaped by sprinting down Aspen streets and alleys.

"Everything now is concentrated on getting him back," said Kienast. "And after that there will be some changes around here (regarding Bundy's custody)." He did not elaborate. Bundy may have tipped his hand about the escape plan. at previous court sessions. according to Whitney Wulff, Kienast's secretary, who at times sat in on the hearings. She said:

"He would walk over to the windows by himself, look down, then glance at sheriff's personnel to watch their reaction. I thought he always was testing us.

"Once he walked up close behind a girl court aide and looked at us. I got worried about the possibility of a hostage and alerted the officer escort to stay closer to the prisoner."

Bundy, formerly of Seattle and Tacoma, is charged with first-degree murder in the death of Michigan nurse Caryn Campbell, 23, near here January 12, 1975.

Deputy Peter Murphy said that when he and Sergeant Rick Kralicek of the Pitkin sheriff's office picked up Bundy at Glenwood Springs, where he was being kept in the Garfield County Jail. For the trip to Aspen Tuesday morning Bundy made small talk.

But as they were leaving Glenwood Springs, Murphy remembered:

"I was in the backseat and Bundy suddenly turned around and stared at me. Then he made several quick motions with his 'cuffed hands. I unsnapped the leather strap holding my 38 revolver in the holster. It was a loud unmistakable snap and he turned around looking straight forward the rest of the trip."

Twice before since being jailed, Bundy led his jailers to believe he was planning an escape.

Last October, Utah penitentiary authorities said they found Bundy in possession of false identification. maps and notes on airline schedules.

About a month ago Garfield County Sheriff Ed Hogue said yesterday, jailers in that county intercepted a plan of the jail that another prisoner was attempting to pass to Bundy.

Bundy claimed, according to Hogue, that he needed the plan for an appeal that he was being denied space equal to other prisoners. But Hogue said the jail plan had all the exits marked.

Bundy had been transferred in April from the Pitkin County Jail in Aspen to the Garfield County Jail in Glenwood Springs because the state health department said the Aspen jail was unfit to hold prisoners for more than 30 days due to inadequate space and lighting and because authorities said the jail afforded poor security.

A prisoner who had been in the Aspen jail with Bundy and then was transferred to Glenwood Springs tried to pass the jail plan to Bundy, Hogue said. That prisoner, Dan Kellum, after serving four or five months of a one-year sentence for theft, had recently been given a reduced sentence and placed on work-release, Hogue said.

A week ago, Kellum failed to return to jail from the work-release, even though he had only 37 days left to serve.

Hogue said he had no idea if Kellum helped Bundy to escape.

But Hogue said he was concerned enough about Bundy's intentions to insist that, when Bundy was in Garfield County, he be placed in leg irons and guarded by two deputies whenever he was out of his cell.

"I figured he had nothing to lose," Hogue said "and, given the opportunity, he was going to try to split."

June 9, 1977
Darkness Falls - and Bundy Is Still Free

ASPEN, Colo. - Escapee Ted Bundy, labelled "desperate and dangerous" by Pitkin County Sheriff Dick Kienast, remained at large yesterday as darkness set in on this mountain resort town.

There were signs the massive two-day manhunt for Bundy, who made a daring leap to freedom from a second- story county courthouse window here Tuesday, was slacking off.

Five of six tracking dogs were called in and a search helicopter stayed on the ground much of the afternoon as the hunt produced no good leads on Bundy's whereabouts.

The scope of the search, conducted by some 150 lawmen and volunteers Tuesday and yesterday, was uncertain today although it will continue.

A felony escape charge will be filed against the fugitive soon, said a deputy district attorney here. If convicted, Bundy could get from five to 40 years.

The last definite clue to Bundy's whereabouts came Tuesday afternoon when dogs tracked him to the Roaring Fork River, east of Aspen.

Denver K-9 officers said Bundy had crossed the river, then recrossed it and walked onto an adjoining hard-surface street in the vicinity of Herron Park. The dogs lost his scent on the pavement.

There was some speculation Bundy could have been picked up by a vehicle there.

Many of the citizens and sheriff's reservists, including mounted posses, taking part in the search looked like something out of a Charles Russell or Frederick Remington painting, with their Stetsons, deerskin vests, jeans, jodhpurs, weathered countenances and shooting irons at their sides.

As house searches in and around Aspen continued. Capt. Dick Wall, head of the Pitkin County Sheriff's Reserves, cautioned his men to be cool and keep another searcher in sight "so you know the guy next to you hasn't been picked up by Bundy."

Some officers have a growing suspicion Bundy, perhaps armed with a gun, remains in town, in a vacant house or perhaps concealed by someone.

The longer Bundy stays at large, the more noticeable is the fear in Aspen, particularly in the dark hours.

Bundy, a suspect in the disappearances or deaths of 18 young women in Colorado and Utah, is charged with murdering Caryn Campbell, 23, a vacationing Michigan nurse, near here January 12, 1975.

He was convicted in Salt Lake City in March 1976 of kidnaping Carol DaRonch, 17, from suburban Murray. She escaped to identify Bundy as her attempted abductor, and he was sentenced to one to 15 years.

Bundy was extradited to Colorado in mid-April of this year and has been confined in the Garfield County Jail, at Glenwood Springs, 42 miles northwest of Aspen. Court hearings on his case are held in Aspen, where his trial in the Campbell murder was scheduled for November 14.

June 10, 1977
Bundy Becomes Part of Folklore

ASPEN, Colo. - Ted Bundy's dramatic escape Tuesday from an antique courthouse here has made him part of the folklore of this summer and winter Rocky Mountain playground.

T-shirts are sprouting out around town with inscriptions about the convicted kidnaper and accused murderer.

One says: "Bundy Is in Booth 'D'."

It alludes to a national magazine article that said if you sit in Booth D in a certain Aspen disco, you will be served cocaine, the "drug of the elite."

One of Aspen's campy eateries has a "Bundy Burger," open it and discover the meat has fled.

A bar is serving a "Bundy 'Cocktail" tequila. rum and two Mexican jumping beans.

Revellers at counter-culture meccas or disco-hopping the streets at night yell out slogans such as, "Bundy Lives - On a

Rocky Mountain High," referring to a favorite number of singer John Denver.

Another slogan:

"Bundy's Free - You can bet your Aspen on it."

Hitchhikers have been seen in the area wearing signs:

"I'm not Bundy."

The escapee is talked of as rivalling famed Seattle jet hijacker D. B. Cooper in Western folklore. But there are many who think this is sick, because D.B. never was charged with killing women or kidnaping them.

It remains to be seen whether the Bundy lore will rival or surpass the publicity generated here by showgirl Claudine Longet's accidental slaying of her pro-skier Spider Sabich here last fall.

The maudlin fun over Bundy's escape contrasts starkly with the serious aspects of his being at large - and the fact he is a suspect in deaths or disappearances of 18 women in three states including eight in King County, Washington State.

Sheriff's officers, red-faced about Bundy escaping from lax security here Tuesday, try to discount any panic among the people. But fear stalks Aspen's storied streets.

This reporter, for example, was turned in to the sheriff's office as a possible Bundy suspect, after talking to three women in a cafe garden to get their reactions to the escape.

They turned the writer in even though he showed press card and other identification.

The only result was razzing for the writer from sheriff's officers and fellow news people.

The controversy continued about lax security that allowed Bundy to bail out of a second-floor window in the courthouse here. Pitkin County Sheriff Dick Kienast was asked:

"Sheriff, do you wish you'd never heard of Ted Bundy?"

"Yes," he replied.

The sheriff said the lone guard on Bundy in the courtroom, Deputy David Westerlund, had specific orders to keep Bundy in sight at all times, but instead was out in the hall during a recess when Bundy bailed out the window using shelves of lawbooks to screen his leap.

The sheriff said District Judge George Lohr, in allowing Bundy to represent himself on the case, also allowed the defendant to be unmanacled, despite the sheriff's earlier getting an order that Bundy wear handcuffs in court.

Judge Lohr yesterday said his recollection of these things is "imperfect." but any order he had given would be shown in the record. A check of the record does not show such an order, but the sheriff said he remembers it as being verbal.

June 10, 1977
Mother To Bundy: Give Up

TACOMA - The mother of Theodore Bundy is pleading with him to give up and says she was afraid searchers would shoot first and ask questions later.

Mrs. Louise Bundy, in an interview with Tacoma station KSTW-TV. said she was worried about her son being out in the mountains of Colorado. "But most of all, I'm worried about the people who are out looking for him not using good common sense and pulling the trigger first and asking questions later."

Mrs. Bundy said she thought her son's escape from a courthouse in Aspen, would hurt his case in Colorado, where Bundy was awaiting trial on a charge of first-degree murder in the slaying of a Michigan nurse, whose nude body was found in 1975.

"People will think, 'oh, he must be guilty, that's why he's running." But I think just all the frustrations piled up and he saw an open window and decided to go. I'm sure by now he's probably sorry he did," said Mrs. Bundy.

June 10, 1977
FBI Enters Bundy Search

ASPEN, Colo. The three-day-old manhunt for escaped murder suspect Ted Bundy went nationwide yesterday as the Federal Bureau of Investigation entered the search.

A scaled-down search for Bundy in and around Aspen continued fruitless yesterday. The number of searchers dropped from 150 to about 70.

In Colorado, at a tunnel on Interstate 70, 50 miles west of Denver, Pitkin County sheriff's officers took into custody Daniel Kellum for questioning as a possible accomplice in Bundy's escape here.

Kellum, 30, a friend and former cellmate of Bundy here, failed to return Friday to the Garfield County jail in Glenwood Springs, 42 miles to the northwest, from work release. He was serving a year for receiving stolen property Both he and Bundy had been transferred to the Garfield jail from the old county jail here.

The FBI entered the hunt, two days after Bundy's escape, when a federal escape warrant was issued on Bundy from Salt Lake City. It charges unlawful fight to avoid confinement for kidnaping.

Kellum was brought into the sheriff's office here at 10 p.m. Seattle time for interrogation.

Sheriff Dick Kienast said that based on the Interrogation. "It does not appear Kellum was involved as an accomplice in Bundy's escape."

However, the sheriff said Kellum confirmed he and Bundy, as jail buddies here, did talk of escape plans. Kienast said Kellum also provided some of his own ideas as to where Bundy might be. He suggested Bundy might be in Pitkin County, but outside of Aspen.

June 11, 1977
Canyon Near Aspen Scoured for Bundy

ASPEN, Colo. - Federal, state and local authorities yesterday pushed a coordinated search for escapee Ted Bundy, 30, who remained at large a fourth day.

The hunt was concentrated in the Hunter Creek area, just northeast of Aspen. A former Bundy cellmate, Daniel Kellum, 30, told interrogators he and Bundy had talked of escaping and hiding out in that canyon, perhaps using old cabins for shelter and provisions. An earlier search of the Hunter Creek canyon, with dogs, was fruitless.

Pitkin County Sheriff Dick Kienast said checks of Aspen homes, vacant and occupied, were resumed yesterday. He added that other areas outside the city in addition to Hunter Creek also will be rechecked.

Kienast said he does not believe Kellum, who failed to report back from work release a week ago, was an accomplice in Bundy's spectacular jump to freedom from a second-floor courtroom here.

Kellum, serving a year for receiving stolen property, was picked up Thursday night working with a road tunnel crew 50 miles west of Denver. He is to appear before a judge here Monday.

Bundy, charged with murdering Michigan nurse Caryn Campbell, 23, near here January 12, 1975, was in court Tuesday for hearing of motions, when he escaped.

A law student at the University of Utah when first arrested in Salt Lake City August 16, 1975, Bundy is a suspect in the deaths or disappearances of 18 women in Colorado, Utah and King County.

Last year he was convicted of kidnaping a young woman near Salt Lake City November 8, 1974. He was serving one to 15 years in Utah State Prison when brought to Colorado last January for trial here November 14 in Miss Campbell's death.

The FBI entered the case Thursday on the basis of a federal escape warrant issued against Bundy from Salt Lake City. A Colorado escape charge also was filed.

The number of searchers in the manhunt has been reduced considerably. But a sheriff's spokesman said, "we are working in ways that won't be as noticeable."

June 12, 1977
Bundy Took Rifle, Ammo In Break-in

ASPEN, Colo. - Theodore Bundy apparently is armed with a rifle which he obtained after breaking into a cabin in the Castle

Creek area about 10 miles southwest of here. the Pitkin County Sheriff's Department said last night.

Nina Johnston, spokeswoman for the sheriff's office, said Bundy's fingerprints were found in the cabin, and it appeared that he had eaten some food and taken the rifle and some ammunition. Officials estimated Bundy had been at the cabin between 48 and 72 hours before, she said.

Trained dogs were flown from Denver last night to assist in the manhunt, which was shifted from the area east of Aspen to the Castle Creek area following the discovery of the break-in earlier yesterday. The use of dogs had been suspended Wednesday after a rain shower caused the dogs to lose Bundy's scent.

Meanwhile, officials were expressing renewed optimism in their search. "We think we are close," said Mrs. Johnston. "This is the only good lead we've had since he escaped."

Friday, the search concentrated in a canyon around Hunter Creek, just northeast of Aspen. A former cellmate of Bundy's, Daniel Kellum, had reported he and Bundy had talked about escaping and hiding out in that canyon.

But a sheriff's spokeswoman said yesterday the search in the Hunter Creek area had been fruitless and searchers were now combing other areas.

Bundy, a former resident of Seattle and Tacoma and a suspect in the deaths and disappearances of eight young women in Western Washington during 1974, was in Colorado to stand trial this fall for murder in the death of a young woman near Aspen.

Last year, he was convicted of kidnaping a young woman near Salt Lake City and sentenced to one to 15 years in prison.

June 13, 1977
Bundy Search Centers in Woods

ASPEN, Colo. - Escaped murder suspect Theodore Bundy remained at large yesterday, as law enforcement officers focused their search in the rugged mountain forests south of Aspen.

Some 20 searchers, aided by tracking dogs and a Rocky Mountain Rescue Team helicopter, were working the Castle

Creek area after Bundy's fingerprints were found in an unoccupied vacation cabin.

A rifle, a parka and some food had been taken from the cabin Thursday or Friday, said District Attorney Frank Tucker.

"We all figured this would escalate if Bundy got a weapon," weapon," said Tucker. "I'm concerned about people up there in their campers and ranchers or vacationers in the summer homes."

Whitney Wulff, a spokeswoman at the Pitkin County sheriff's office, said, "Castle Creek is a tourist area, with a lot of good spots if (Bundy) followed the trails. Survival should be relatively easy for him."

She said the dogs had been used to follow the trail from the cabin, "but lost the trail after about 50 feet."

Sgt. Don Davis of the sheriff's department said last night it also is believed that Bundy may have taken a small transistor radio when he broke into the cabin. Because of that possibility, sheriff's reports to the news media about areas being searched will be sketchy from now on, the sergeant said.

"We're not sure he has that radio." Davis said. "But we don't want to talk to him if he does."

Bundy, 30, from Tacoma, escaped from the Pitkin County Courthouse law library Tuesday, after jumping more than 25 feet from a second-floor window.

Bundy was transferred from the Utah State Prison to stand trial for the January 1975 death of Caryn Campbell, a vacationing Michigan nurse. Bundy had been serving a 1-to-15-year sentence for kidnaping a Salt Lake City girl in 1974.

"He's headed into very rugged, even primitive territory he is not familiar with," said Tucker. "I think Bundy is still on foot. He now has food, a parka and a deer rifle, but I don't know if he has any ammunition."

June 14, 1977
Weary Bundy Rests in Cell

An exhausted and heavily guarded Theodore R. Bundy yesterday slept off the effects of wandering for six wet and cold days while eluding hundreds of searchers in the mountains around Aspen, Colo.

Bundy, convicted of kidnaping and accused of murder, was captured early yesterday, ending an escapade that began when he jumped from the second-story window of the Pitkin County Courthouse in Aspen a week ago today.

No one was watching him when he escaped; yesterday he was guarded by a whole squad of sheriff's deputies.

Deputies Maureen Higgins and Gene Flatt captured Bundy at 2 a.m. yesterday on the cast outskirts of Aspen. He was driving a stolen car and wearing a crude disguise that didn't fool the two young officers.

The deputies at first thought they had a drunk driver because the auto was moving erratically.

Although he earlier took a rifle and ammunition from a mountain cabin, Bundy offered no resistance when spreadeagled on the ground and searched. He said he had ditched the weapon when he stole the car in hopes of driving out of Aspen.

"He was a very tired Ted Bundy," said Whitney Wulff, Sheriff Dick Kienast's secretary, "but he managed to wink at me and other women after they brought him in.

Bundy, a 30-year-old former resident of Seattle and Tacoma, had lost about 20 pounds and walked with a limp caused by an injury while hiding in the hills. He also had bruises and scratches from running through the brush.

Whereas no guard was in the courtroom when Bundy fled on Tuesday, yesterday when he was taken back into the same court. room, deputies were everywhere.

Ms. Wulff said there were five guards in the courtroom, including one in a law library area from which Bundy made his jump: three outside the court. room and four others "securing' the area.

Bundy wore wrist chains to the courtroom and leg irons once he was inside. He had neither when he escaped.

District Judge George Lohr read the captured fugitive his rights and told him he will be prosecuted for felony escape, as well as felony and misdemeanor theft and first-degree burglary. The latter charges stem from Bundy's breaking into the Castle

Creek arca cabin and taking items, plus theft of the 1966 Cadillac he was caught in.

Bundy will be arraigned on the new charges Thursday.

In the murder case, set for trial November 14, he is charged with killing Michigan nurse Caryn Campbell, 23, near Aspen Jan. 12, 1975.

Bundy, when extradited to Colorado last January, was serving 1-15 years in Utah State Prison after being convicted of kidnaping a young woman near Salt Lake City on Nov. 8, 1974.

He also is a main suspect in deaths and disappearances of 17 other young women in Utah. Colorado and King County, Washington dating from early 1974.

Bundy told officers that after jumping out the courthouse window Tuesday. he ran to the Roaring Fork River, east of town. waited near a bridge a while, then ran up a street and on up Aspen Mountain, south of town.

He reached the Castle Creek area, about six miles out of Aspen, that afternoon, passed the cabin and headed up Conundrum Creek valley. It rained that evening and Bundy spent a cold, wet and miserable night in the open.

He went back to the cabin Wednesday, spending the night there, and left Thursday, crossing into the East Maroon valley. There, he became disoriented. so went back to the cabin by Saturday He realized officers had been there, investigating his break-in and thefts of the rifle and food, so he slept outside Saturday night.

Extremely exhausted, he headed back toward Aspen Sunday and stole the auto, with keys in the ignition, in the west part of town. He tried to drive over Independence Pass, southeast of Aspen, but the road was blocked by a slide.

He reversed his course and was driving west when the two officers spotted him.

Bundy was driving erratically and was slumped down in the seat.

He wore a plaid shirt. yellow fishing hat, wire rim glasses and a Band-Aid on his nose, none of which he wore when he escaped. However, he wore the same boots, which are from the Utah prison.

Ms. Wulff said the Colorado Bureau of Investigation is investigating the circumstances of Bundy's escape and no disciplinary action against officers responsible will be taken until the probe is completed.

The lone deputy guarding Bundy in the courtroom, David Westerlund, was in the hall during a recess in the hearing, when Bunly went out the window. Sheriff Kienast said officers had standing orders to keep Bundy in sight at all times.

June 15, 1977
Bundy's Escape No Impulse...

Theodore R. Bundy said he planned to escape for months, but had definitely decided to try it on June 7, the day he leaped to freedom from a second-story courthouse window in Aspen, Colo., sheriff's officers there said yesterday.

Bundy, charged with murdering a woman near Aspen Jan. 12. 1975, made the admissions under interrogation by Colorado Bureau of Identification and Pitkin County sheriff's officers.

A map of the area around Aspen was found in the pocket of a coat Bundy had early Monday. when he was recaptured in a stolen car in the east outskirts of Aspen.

Colleen Curtis, a sheriff's spokeswoman, said:

"Bundy told interrogators that when he was picked up at the Garfield County jail in Glenwood Springs for the trip to Aspen June 7 (for a court' hearing), he had decided to escape that day. The unguarded courthouse window provided the opportunity."

Ms. Curtis said Bundy, exhausted at the time of his capture by six days in the nearby mountains. "Looks a lot better today." following a good night's sleep in a jail cell and hot food.

He will be arraigned on escape and theft charges tomorrow, then will be returned to the Garfield County jail.

Bundy, convicted of kidnaping a girl near Salt Lake City in 1974, still is scheduled to stand trial in Aspen November 14 for the murder of Michigan nurse Caryn Campbell at a nearby ski resort.

June 17, 1977
Bundy Gets a New Attorney

Theodore R. Bundy got a new attorney yesterday as the murder defendant was arraigned in Aspen, Colo., on new charges of escape, theft and burglary, stemming from his recent escape.

Aspen lawyer Stephen Ware was appointed by District Judge George Lohr to represent Bundy after the judge allowed Public Defenders Charles Leidner and James Dumas to withdraw.

Leidner and Dumas said they will be called as witnesses against Bundy on the escape charges, because they were in the courtroom. from which Bundy escaped June 7. He was captured in a stolen car in Aspen after eluding searchers for six days in the nearby mountains.

The two public defenders had served in an advisory role because Bundy has been representing himself, and will continue to do so, against charges he murdered Michigan nurse Caryn Campbell near Aspen Jan. 12, 1975.

Ware will represent Bundy on the escape, theft and burglary charges and apparently serve in an advisory role on the murder charge. The murder trial is scheduled for November 14.

Judge Lohr set a preliminary hearing on the new charges for next Thursday. The theft and burglary charges accuse Bundy of breaking into a mountain cabin while free and taking items, including a 22-caliber rifle; he is also accused of stealing the car in which he was caught.

Attorney Ware is noted in the Aspen area for his defense of narcotics cases.

A sheriff's officer said Bundy was to be taken to the Garfield County jail in Glenwood Springs, 42 miles northwest of Aspen, late yesterday.

Bundy, formerly of Seattle and Tacoma Had been kept in the antiquated Pitkin County Jail in Aspen since his recapture Monday. He was under heavy security. especially during court appearances. He was being kept in the Garfield jail before his escape and was transported to Aspen for court hearings.

Bundy, a suspect in deaths and disappear of 18 women, is serving one to 15 years for a Utah kidnaping conviction.

June 30, 1977
Bundy Flight Fallout: Five Deputies Quit

Five deputies, including the undersheriff, have resigned following Theodore R. Bundy's June 7 escape and recapture in Aspen, Colo., Pitkin County Sheriff Dick Kienast said yesterday.

Kienast said the resignations, not all directly connected to the escape, followed an investigation of the matter by the Colorado Bureau of Investigation.

Two of the resignations, the sheriff said, were direct results of the escape. Deputy David Westerlund, the report says, let Bundy out of his sight by going out into the hall during a court hearing recess. Bundy then jumped 25 feet from a second-story window.

Sgt. Rick Kralicek, as shift commander, should have been aware of the courtroom security problem, the report said. Kralicek and a second deputy brought Bundy to the courtroom and left him in Westerlund's custody.

Kralicek quit June 21 and Westerlund June 24.

Kienast said the resignations of Undersheriff Ben Meyers and another sergeant and a deputy he did not name, were for "personal reasons" only remotely connected with Bundy's escape.

The sheriff said a CBI report listed these other reasons for Bundy's escape:

The courtroom, with 10 windows and three doors, is an insecure place and Bundy told interrogators he had been determined to escape that day. Only physical restraint would have stopped him.

The policy of the court (of District Judge George Lohr) was that defendants not be restrained in his courtroom. Bundy wore no handcuffs or leg irons.

Bundy, formerly of Tacoma and Seattle, eluded searchers for six days in the mountains around Aspen before being recaptured trying to drive a stolen auto through town. He now wears restraints in court.

The 30-year-old former law student. political worker and state employee at Olympia is charged with murdering a Michigan nurse Jan. 12. 1975, near Aspen. He was convicted of kidnaping a woman near Salt Lake City in 1974 and is serving 1-15 years in Utah State Prison for that offense. Bundy also is a suspect in the disappearances and deaths of a number of women in King County, Utah and Colorado.

He will appear next in the courtroom on July 14, to continue hearings on motions in the murder case. His preliminary hearing on escape charges will be July 29. His murder trial is scheduled November 14.

October 12, 1977
Bundy Probers to Exhume Slain Girl's Body

Utah authorities plan to exhume the body of Laura Ann Aime, 17, beaten to death in that state three years ago in a case in which Ted Bundy is a suspect.

Utah County Attorney Noal Wooton was quoted by the Associated Press from Provo as saying that a court request to exhume the girl's body signalled a "break" in the case, but he wouldn't say what it was.

It appeared, however, that investigators hope to match scalp hair from the exhumed body with samples taken from a Volkswagen bug owned by Bundy when he was a law student at the University of Utah in Salt Lake City in 1975.

Bundy, charged with murdering Caryn Campbell, 23, a Michigan nurse, near Aspen, Colo., in 1975, is to go on trial in Aspen January 4. He is in jail in Glenwood Springs, Colo.

The former Tacoma and Seattle resident, who has been investigated in a series of deaths of young women in King County and in Utah and Colorado, was convicted in 1975 of kidnaping Carol DaRonch, 17, from a Salt Lake City suburb.

She escaped and identified Bundy at the trial as her kidnaper. He was given a prison sentence of from one to 15 years, but an appeals court has ordered the trial court to examine new evidence and determine if it warrants a new trial. Bundy's attorney claims a document shows DaRonch was "programmed" by police to identify Bundy but that she actually wasn't certain he was her abductor.

The hearing on this matter has been rescheduled from Friday to October 31.

Ms. Aime vanished the night of Oct. 31, 1974, after stepping out of her home in Lehi, south of Salt Lake City. Her nude, beaten body was found nearly a month later in nearby American Fork Canyon.

When Bundy was arrested in Salt Lake City in the DaRonch kidnaping in 1975, sheriff's officers seized the VW, which he had sold, and vacuumed it for evidence.

Various hair samples were found, and the Federal Bureau of Investigation lab has said some of the samples matched hair of Ms. Campbell, Ms. DaRonch and Melissa Smith, 17, of Midvale, Utah, who disappeared in 1974 and whose body was found later near Midvale.

Yesterday, Brent Bullock, a deputy county attorney at Provo, said both the FBI and Colorado Bureau of Identification labs have requested hair samples from Ms. Aime's body.

Bullock indicated some samples had already been submitted to the labs but that they asked for more. He refused to speculate that this meant a "match" could be made of hair bits found in Bundy's auto and samples turned in to the labs.

But he said his county's investigation of the Aime case was progressing satisfactorily.

October 26, 1977
New Move On Bundy By Utah Prosecutor

Colo. - Special Prosecutor Milton Blakey has filed sealed evidence he claims links former Tacoman Theodore Bundy with a slaying and the disappearance of two 17-year-old girls in Utah in 1974.

District Court Judge George Lohr will hear arguments Nov 2.

The filing by Blakey is part of the legal maneuvering preliminary to Bundy's trial for the January 1975 slaying of a Michigan nurse. Caryn Campbell. Miss Campbell was vacationing at Snowmass near Aspen when she was slain.

Blakey filed a notice of intent Sept. 7 that he will try to link Bundy with the murder of Laura Ann Aime of Salem, Utah, whose body was found Nov. 27, 1974. after she was missing a week.

The prosecutor said he also would try to show that Bundy was involved in the disappearance of Debra Kent from a parking lot near Viewmont High School in Bountiful, Utah, in 1974.

Bundy, who is defending himself, said there is no connection among the cases. Lohr gave both sides a week to submit briefs, prior to the Nov 2 date.

November 8, 1977
Utah Evidence Ruled Out of Bundy Trial

Evidence in two 1974 Utah slayings cannot be admitted into the Colorado murder trial of Ted Bundy, a judge in Aspen. Colo., has ruled.

District Judge George C Lohr said Special Prosecutor Milton Blakey's offer of proof failed to connect Bundy with the two Utah cases.

Blakey, using a "similar transactions" strategy, had attempted a link Bundy with the murder of Laura Ann Aime, 17, and the disappearance of Debra Kent, also 17, in the Salt Lake City area.

Bundy is scheduled to stand trial January 4 in Aspen for the 1975 slaying near there of Michigan nurse Caryn Campbell.

He was convicted in 1975 in Salt Lake City of the 1974 kidnaping of Carol DaRonch, 17, who escaped to identify Bundy as her abductor. Bundy is seeking a new trial in that case on grounds police withheld information that Ms. DaRonch "wasn't a good witness".

Blakey will attempt to use evidence in the DaRonch case as part of the Colorado case against Bundy. Judge Lohr's ruling did not apply to that case.

November 15, 1977
Testimony On Bundy's Car

ASPEN, Colo. - A silk stocking and a ski mask were found during a search of Theodore Bundy's car the summer after the body of a Michigan nurse was discovered near here, law enforcement officers said yesterday.

Six Utah officers told an evidentiary hearing in district court that the items were found and confiscated after Bundy's car was stopped in Midvale, Utah for a traffic violation.

Bundy, a former law student and resident of Tacoma and Seattle, appeared at the hearing in a dark blue prison suit jumpsuit and wearing leg shackles.

He is accused of the January 1975 murder of Caryn Campbell, a Dearborn, Mich. Nurse who was vacationing in Aspen when she disappeared Her nude, frozen body was found a month later in a snowbank beside a rural road Bundy has been extradited to Colorado from Utah, where he is serving a 1-to-15-year sentence for the 1974 kidnapping of a Salt Lake City girl.

At yesterday's hearing, the officers said Bundy gave them permission to look in his car. But an attorney for Bundy contended that Bundy's permission did not constitute approval for a search of the vehicle.

The defense counsel told the court he would attempt to show that the initial search of Bundy's car and a subsequent search of his apartment were conducted illegally His attorneys want the evidence from those searches to be ruled inadmissible at his upcoming trial, scheduled for January.

Yesterday's testimony opened what is expected to be a lengthy hearing on what evidence may be introduced at Bundy's trial.

The police officers said that the stocking and mask, along with a crowbar, were taken from the vehicle when it was stopped in August. 1975. At the time. they said, Bundy told them he had never been to Colorado.

But during the following search of Bundy's apartment, the officers said, a Colorado map, a brochure on Colorado ski country, and a credit card slip were confiscated.

November 17, 1977
Witness Questioned by Bundy

ASPEN, Colo - Theodore Bundy, accused of murder and acting in his own defense, in an effort to suppress evidence for his forthcoming trial, yesterday spent two hours cross examining a Utah woman he was convicted of kidnaping three years ago.

Carol DaRonch of Murray, Utah. was calm throughout the questioning, although she was unable to remember some specific details of her Nov. 8 1974 abduction from a shopping center parking lot.

Earlier in the day proceedings had been brought to an abrupt halt when Bundy scuffled with deputies and broke his lightweight chain leg restraints. He was escorted downstairs to the jail but reappeared at the afternoon session in the usual leg restraints.

Bundy, who faces trial in January for the 1975 murder of Caryn Campbell, a vacationing Michigan nurse, was convicted in Utah of the DaRonch kidnaping, but maintains his innocence and is appealing the conviction.

He and his attorneys want to block evidence from the DaRonch case, as well as the murder of a Utah woman. Melissa Smith, from being introduced at his trial for the Campbell killing Prosecutors are attempting to show similarities in the circumstances surrounding DaRonch's abduction and Campbell's death.

DaRonch testified yesterday that she had identified Bundy with certainty, and without any suggestions from Utah law enforcement officers She said she had identified Bundy by the way he had walked onto the stage during a police lineup.

Bundy prefaced his cross-examination by asking DaRonch to relax, assuring her that he was not there to upset her. He asked numerous questions about her observations during the abduction about the car and about all circumstances surrounding the event.

November 22, 1977
Bundy Plea for New Trial Denied

A judge in Salt Lake City Monday denied Ted Bundy's motion for a new trial on his 1976 Utah kidnapping conviction.

Bundy, who got 1-15 years in prison for the 1974 abduction of Carol DaRonch, then 17, maintained police withheld information that they believed DaRonch was a "poor witness."

But District Judge Jay Banks said Bundy's contention was untrue and the disputed information wouldn't have changed the outcome of the trial anyway. Bundy is awaiting trial in Aspen, Colo., where he is charged with the 1975 murder of Michigan nurse Caryn Campbell.

That trial is scheduled to begin January 4. In pretrial hearings Monday in Aspen, the prosecution sought permission to introduce evidence concerning other crimes at the trial.

January 1, 1978
Bundy Escapes Again

Ted Bundy, prime suspect in disappearances or deaths of 18 women in three states, yesterday fled his jail cell in Glenwood Springs, Colo. - his second escape in six months.

Roadblocks were set up and search parties were combing the area for Bundy, 30, who was to go on trial in Colorado Springs Jan. 9 in the 1975 murder near Aspen of vacationing Michigan nurse Caryn Campbell, 23.

Bundy had been in the jail nine months.

Bundy was discovered missing around noon yesterday when a deputy sheriff found blankets rolled up in Bundy's bunk to make it appear the prisoner was in bed.

Garfield County Undersheriff Robert A. Hart said Bundy escaped by removing the light fixture in his cell and crawling up through the foot-square hole into the jail building's attic.

From the attic, Bundy came down into the apartment of head jailer Bob Morrison, then walked free out the front door of the jail building, Hart said. Morrison and his wife were absent from their apartment for some time Friday night and yesterday forenoon.

Bundy took two weapons, a rifle and derringer, from Morrison's apartment, and put them in the attic. Hart said the working replicas of old-time weapons had been recovered. Both were muzzle-loaders.

The undersheriff said Bundy, wearing blue Levis, a grey turtleneck sweater and tennis shoes, is not known to be armed.

Bundy escaped the county. courthouse at Aspen June 7 by jumping out a second-story window. He was captured five days later in Aspen after spending his free days and nights in the nearby hills.

Hart said he doubts Bundy would take to the hills again.

"We got six inches of fresh snow last night; we've had a foot or more before that and the temperatures get down below freezing," he explained.

"Bundy couldn't take the chill in the hills around Aspen in June, so I don't think he would try it around here in December," the undersheriff said.

Hart said there is a possibility Bundy had arranged to have someone in a car pick him up in Glenwood Springs when he escaped.

"We're dealing with a highly intelligent person. He would have this escape worked out thoroughly," Hart said.

"Bundy had unlimited use of the telephone. He had a credit card to place calls wherever he wanted. And the court ordered us not to listen in on his calls..." "Hell, he could have called President Carter over in Europe if he was of a mind to do it..."

Bundy was given a telephone, the use of law libraries, and other privileges because he is defending himself against the Campbell murder charges.

The victim's nude, frozen body was found three miles from a ski resort near Aspen in January, 1975. She was vacationing with her fiancée, a physician, and had gone to her room to get a magazine after dining. She was never seen alive again.

Gasoline credit card slips placed Bundy in the area of this slaying and two others in Colorado, officials have reported.

Bundy says he is innocent of these slayings and several in Utah that prosecutors have sought to connect him with.

He also is the prime suspect in the deaths or disappearances of eight Pacific Northwest women the first half of 1974, according to law enforcement officials here. Skeletal remains of six of these victims were found at two sites near Issaquah. Authorities in the three states say Bundy is the prime suspect in the eight Washington cases and five each in Utah and Colorado.

Bundy was convicted of kidnaping Carol DaRonch, then 17, from a Salt Lake City suburb in November 1974, and got from 1-15 years in Utah State Prison. He has appealed.

A former resident of Tacoma and Seattle, Bundy was a campaign worker for former Gov. Dan Evans in 1972 and worked in the state Republican Party organization. He also held a job in the state Department of Emergency Services at Olympia in 1974.

TO BE CONTINUED....